—⁕—

Tell 'Em Who You Are!

A Life in the West of Ireland

—⁕—

Dick Byrne

BALLYHAY BOOKS

Published by Ballyhay Books,
an imprint of Laurel Cottage Ltd.
Donaghadee, N. Ireland 2008.
Copyrights Reserved.
© Text by Dick Byrne 2008.
All rights reserved.
No part of this book may be reproduced
or stored on any media without the express
written permission of the publishers.
Printed by Gutenberg Press Ltd., Malta.

ISBN 978 1 900935 73 9

Written in
Craughwell, Co. Galway and Puisserguier, France

for Richard, Derval
and my beloved Dorothy

Contents

—∭—

1. Always Play the Game

—ᴍ—

Iwasn't born in time for the First World War. I arrived seventeen years after that one. I wasn't even born in time for the second one either, (known as the Emergency in our part of Ireland) although I did arrive four years before it began, I was only nine when it all ended. What has this got to do with anything? Surely I couldn't have any interest in the First World War, let alone the second one. Well, you see, I have in a way. It has all to do with my paternal grandfather, Richard Eugene Byrne, soldier, drill instructor and something of a martinet.

I was the first grandson in the male line. Although I had male and female first cousins who were older than me, they were his daughter's children. I was the first and, as it turned out, the only grandchild in the male succession, my father being yet another Richard Byrne. If you add this to the fact that I was born on the eleventh day of the eleventh month, which was the anniversary of the 1914-18 Armistice Day, he couldn't have been more chuffed. He bragged about this a lot to his old soldier companions; "The lad was born on armistice day, y'know". Afterwards my poor mother told me that she was literally holding on with her legs crossed so that I would make it into the world on the 11th, which I did by about fifteen minutes.

Since this was St Martin's day, in the ordinary way it might have been expected that I would be called Martin, but this was not for me. To put the icing on the cake, I was called Richard not after my father, although the name was the same, but to honour my grandfather. To jump forward I called my son Richard too but he, wisely, put an end to this tradition himself when naming his first and subsequent sons.

My grandfather lived in a small three-bedroom house in Long Walk, by the riverside in Galway City and from the time that I could walk unaided I was paraded down to his house every Sunday morning after mass for inspection. This included nails, ears, neck and boots, all of which had to shine as brightly as if I too was in some tiny children's army. Following inspection I was kitted out for our walk, or to be more correct, march. This took the form of a brisk walk in company with Granda, my cousins and the cocker spaniels, Sport and Flush, around to the docks, across the gates and onto the railway track, which in those days came right down to the quayside. Once at the railway line we would then proceed along the track, walking on the sleepers, in the general direction of Renmore Barracks. The railway sleepers were about two feet apart, which was fine for him, a shortish man, used to marching, but for me they were a stretch and from time to time I would moan a bit, but I soon learned that this was a pointless exercise and so I just put up with it.

As I got older, we could finally make it to Renmore Barracks at full march, which was probably only about a mile and half in each direction, but for a small boy it seemed interminable. When we reached the barracks I would be told all about it, what it was like to live in there, how he and his regiment had been so happy there, the campaigns they went on and how they had to behave when soldiering, until I probably knew more about the Connacht Rangers and soldiering than most young men three times my age. Mind you by this time the Connacht Rangers were long gone, disbanded at least sixteen years, and the First (Irish-speaking) Infantry Battalion of the Irish army was installed in its place. Granda didn't regard those green-uniformed free-state men as real soldiers at all. What did they know about fighting or war? Nothing and besides, he thought, they were very sloppily turned out in their so-called bull's wool uniforms. In fact a few of them had originally been Connacht Rangers, but naturally he wasn't referring to them.

Granda was a short man, about five foot eight or nine, slightly rotund by the time I knew him but in perfect physical shape, or so he kept telling me. He walked very erect, shoulders back, chest out, and stomach as far in as he could manage. His bearing was that of a military man, which had the effect of making him look somewhat taller than he really was. He wore a toothbrush moustache, and tended to purse his lips when in contemplation. He wore a black bowler hat, a dark suit with waistcoat and watch chain exposed, starched collars and immaculately pressed trousers. On returning from his sorties into town he carried a neatly folded newspaper tucked tightly under his arm in the manner of a swagger stick.

He never walked anywhere, he strode. He had that certain pomposity that old soldiers, especially old sergeant majors always had, and in many ways, appearance and style, he greatly resembled Captain Mainwaring of the hilarious *Dad's Army* television series. He never seemed to treat me like a child, but spoke to me in a terse, direct manner, which suggested somebody explaining something to somebody who should know it already. He used old-fashioned English public-school type statements, like "Its just not cricket, boy," if something was wrong and "Jolly good, young man," if it was right, or when giving me advice would tell me, "Always play the game, boy", although I was, for a long time, not sure what game he had in mind. Whenever birthdays or Christmas came along, I was inevitably given boys' books and annuals, with messages such as; "Keep the flag flying, boy", and signed R. E. B., never Granda.

Known as the Bogeyman, Granda was the last regimental Sergeant Major/Warrant Officer of the 2nd Connacht Rangers and fiercely proud of the fact. When young, he had run away from a fairly well-to-do family in Dundrum in Dublin, to come to Galway and join up with the Connacht Rangers. This was primarily, I should imagine, for the adventure, as in those days the British army travelled the world keeping the Empire in line, and soldiers and sailors in Her Majesty's service got to do exciting things and see exciting places.

In 1895 he soldiered as a corporal in India. Again in 1897 and '98 he campaigned as a sergeant with the 2nd Connacht Rangers in Tirah and the Punjab Frontier. By 1902 he was in Africa dealing with the Boers, seeing action in the Transvaal, the Orange Free State and the Cape Colony. It was after these engagements that he returned for a while to Galway where he met and married my grandmother, Winifred Cavanagh (whom I never met as she died twenty years before I was born). He wasn't stationed in Galway City though and was moved about from barracks to barracks, as his first born, May, arrived on the scene in 1906 when he was stationed in Ballinasloe, Co Galway. My father was born in Boyle, Co. Roscommon on the 1st July 1907. There were two further daughters – Kathleen (Ka) and Frances (Fanny).

The so-called Great War for Civilisation saw him back in action, firstly as a Company Sergeant Major, and ultimately as a Warrant Officer 2nd Class. The first few years of that conflict he spent in Ireland as a training sergeant with the 5th Battalion Connaught Rangers, then in Kilworth in England where they were part of the 10th Irish Division and then back in the Curragh in Ireland in 1915. He joined the regiment in the field sometime around the 1st January 1916 as he served with them in Salonika in Greece in that year from 30th September to 2nd October in the Karanjaikos, and on 3rd and 4th October in the capture of Yenikoi.

In September 1917 they were redeployed to Egypt and from 1st to 7th November were involved in the Third Battle of Gaza, where on 6th November, they captured the Sheria position. On 9th December they went on to capture Jerusalem, and on 27th December were involved again in the defence of Jerusalem against a counter attack. In 1918 from 8th to 12th March they fought at Tell A'sur.

Later that same month the 5th left the 10th Division and were transferred to the western front in France where they were attached to the 14th Division, and in July were transferred to the 197th Infantry Brigade in the 66th Division and were involved in the now famous Battle of Cambrai and the pursuit of the German army in retreat to the Selle and from 17th to 25th October in the Battle of the Selle. They were made ready to advance into Germany having advanced through Belgium. They did not advance into Germany though as the signing of the armistice intervened.

Having survived all of that action unscathed he finally came home in one piece, and collected his chest full of medals in the process, a fact of which he was very proud. Of course, for many years afterwards this meant that anyone who would listen, especially young grandsons, would hear these tales of daring-do over and over again. In the end I practically felt that I had been there myself, and have as a result an abiding interest in the First World War in particular.

It is worth mentioning that all of the soldiers in that terrible conflict who hailed from Ireland were volunteers, as conscription was not applied in this island, and yet tens of thousands of them from every side of the political divide went on to fight and die during this brutal conflict, a fact that is often sidelined by armchair historians of the intervening years, particularly those in Northern Ireland who seem to forget that their Southern brothers soldiered and died shoulder to shoulder with them regardless of politics or religion.

Not long after this the Rangers were stood down and he, following a few years of peaceful soldiering, was demobbed. In the thirties he became a school drillmaster, a function that he carried on for many years in the Jesuit College (Boys) and the Dominican College (Girls) in Galway City. Many of his students told me afterwards how tough he was on them and how he was never satisfied until they could drill with the precision and stamina of real soldiers. At this time he was known as the Bogeyman, although I also heard him referred to as Captain Ginger. He got this name, apparently, from a music hall song with which he would occasionally regale the Galway concert audience.

He became known as the Bogeyman during his military service because, when drilling his men he would say; "When you were little lads your mothers would frighten you with tales of the Bogeyman who'll come and get you, you should have listened to her because she was right, I am that Bogeyman, I can see everything and if you don't do what I tell you, you can rest assured that I will personally come and get you".

During the Second World War, especially after the Normandy landings, our house was awash with maps supplied I think with *The Daily Mail,* the only newspaper that either he or my father ever read. These maps were pinned up on the wall of our spare room, and covered the European theatre of war. There were various coloured stickers to indicate the allied forces and the axis forces. Great care was given to marking the various movements of these troops. Much discussion would take place between my father and Granda on strategies etc. and there would be great elation at any allied advance.

Fortunately, he lived long enough to see his side win the European war. He died shortly afterwards in 1945. Had he been young enough, I feel certain that he would have gone back into the affray again. He was very proud when his eldest grandson John Kelly went and joined the Royal Marine Commando. He felt that Ireland was ungrateful for maintaining neutrality, particularly in the matter of their not allowing the allies the use of the ports, but I think he understood deep down that entering the war would have been bad for Ireland. He would have remembered that he and his comrades came home from the First World War only to be treated by and large as traitors.

For many years afterwards when I was a young man, older men would say to me, "Aren't you the Bogeyman's grandson?" I never denied it since his first and foremost bon mot to me was, "Tell 'em who you are, boy". He was proud of who and what he was and I figured that I should be proud of that too.

2. My Father

—ᴍ—

My father, Richard Joseph Byrne, was a completely different sort of person. He was a peaceful man unless riled and not at all like his father. I suppose he had had enough talk of war, soldiers and soldiering in his life since, apart from his father, three of his uncles were in the Services.

His uncle Martin Henry Cavanagh (known for some reason as Christy) was killed in Africa in 1904 while serving as a sailor in the Royal Navy on *HMS Hyacinth*. His party went ashore on an engagement and was involved in the capture of Illig Village in Somalia, or Somaliland as it was then. During an encounter with the Dervishes he was killed in action and buried at sea on 22nd April. His uncle Mike was a gunner in the Royal Navy and fought in many worthwhile naval engagements in the First World War until he was discharged with deafness and part blindness. Their brother, my father's handsome uncle Johnny, came home from America to enlist with the Irish Guards after the outbreak of the First World War and fought on the Somme in 1916 at Flers-Courcelette, the Battle of Morval and the capture of Lesboeufs.

He was wounded several times by gunfire but still went back to the front, where he was finally killed on 26th August 1917.

Dad was a quiet, conservative man, who liked the peaceful life. He was interested in things technical at an early age and I think that it was this interest that gave rise to his first and only brush with crime. He knocked around with the son of a local shopkeeper called Johnno, (who in later life was to embrace the legal trade) and they were very much taken with this new motoring craze. There was a well-to-do chemist in Galway at the time called Wallace who was the very proud possessor of a shiny new Model T Ford car. Although he only lived about half a mile away, on Sunday mornings Mr Wallace would drive proudly down into Eyre Square and park his vehicle prominently outside the Imperial Hotel before heading off on foot to the Augustinians to go to Mass. The boys would take this opportunity to go and examine the car from top to bottom and soon knew every thing there was to know about it, how to start and stop it, how to switch it on, how to turn on the petrol and any other number of technical details.

One Sunday, the temptation got too much for them and, since there was nobody around, they decided to take it for a little drive, just a couple of hundred yards to get the feel of it, and so, as soon as Wallace had gone around the corner they climbed aboard and took off. Things went well, too well in fact, and Johnno decided that they had time to go out as far as the racecourse. Needless to mention they stalled the car out there and flooded the engine and were a long time trying to re-start it. By the time they arrived back on Eyre Square they could see, from a long way off, an irate Wallace waving his stick about and dancing up and down with temper. Now that the car was only moving slowly, Johnno, more afraid of his father than Wallace decided that prudence was the better move and jumped out, leaving my father to change seats and struggle to bring this mechanical beast to a halt. By the time he succeeded Wallace was on him, beating him about the back and head with his stick until he too made a run for it.

Arriving home, he was marked on the face and head and his father wanted to know what exactly had happened to him. Knowing that

Wallace had recognised him and knowing that the story would soon get back to his father, Dad decided to come clean and tell his tale to Granda. The first thing that happened of course was that he had to face another hiding from his father but then the old man, bristling with rage, headed for the Imperial Hotel to confront Wallace whom he knew would be on his second whiskey by now. He stormed in and asked Wallace to come outside and the chemist, not so brave now, did so very reluctantly. When outside, Granda told Wallace that he agreed my father had behaved in an unacceptable manner and apologised for that, but warned him that if he ever, ever laid a hand on his son again he would have him to answer to. A chastened Wallace mumbled an apology and the incident was over.

My father, and probably his father also, decided that a technical career might not be a bad thing for him. Soon he became engrossed with the newly emerging power source, electricity and, having obtained the appropriate preliminary training in Galway's Technical School, he went on to serve his time as an apprentice electrician with the Galway Electrical Company. To earn a few bob on the side he used to sit in as a technical assistant in the orchestra pit at the Old Vic Cinema Theatre to provide the special effects and pyrotechnical explosions for the silent movies. His favourite of all time was *The Four Horsemen of the Apocalypse* as he used to have to spend well over an hour wiring all of the charges and had to rehearse with the orchestra to get the timing of the explosions right. He often commented that after the film, the cinema was filled with smoke and smelt of explosive, adding an extra dimension to the realism of the film; you felt you had actually been in the war.

The Galway Electrical Company was a privately owned company and operated a D.C. (direct current) service for Galway city, which was powered by a great bronze turbine on the river Corrib at Newtownsmith. He became one of their first fully qualified electricians. The burgeoning state-owned E.S.B., or Electricity Supply Board, which had the job of bringing electricity to the whole country, eventually swallowed up the G.E.C. and other private electrical companies. Soon my father found himself employed by the state and riding a large, red Indian motorcycle with a side car that could carry two linesmen and their tools, blasting up and down the highways of Mayo from Westport to Ballyhaunis connecting and maintaining the supply of electricity in those towns. It was in Westport in 1934 that he first met my mother, Jeannie, the seventeen-year-old musician daughter of Harriet and Johnny Clampett, ostler, hotelier, one-time mail coach driver/contractor and a teller of tall tales.

They were immediately attracted to each other, although there was some opposition at first to their alliance he being a Catholic and she being a Protestant. The opposition came particularly from my aunt Gracie's husband Arthur who, though friendly and generally a decent man, was quite bigoted in his way and militantly anti-Catholic, and felt that the marriage was somehow dragging the family name into disrepute. Their love persisted however and they were married in February of the following year. It is worth mentioning that Arthur eventually came to accept the whole affair and couldn't have been nicer to us when we came to stay in Westport. After their wedding they were posted to Castlebar and it was there that I arrived in the world on 11th November 1935.

I never got the chance though to become a citizen of Castlebar, because by the time I was six months old my father was transferred back to Galway City and it was there he was based for the rest of his life, much to his delight and to the delight of my grandfather as well. My mother was also pleased to be away from what was then a small backward country town with nothing much going on. She loved living amidst the hustle and bustle of a city such as it was and, apart from being a new wife and mother, she soon found herself back working at her life's other passion; her music, which she had learned initially from a Mrs ffrench Mayock in Westport and subsequently in the very refined Mercers' boarding school for Protestant girls in Dublin.

Our first apartment or 'flat' as they were then called, was a two bedroom, sitting room, kitchen unit in Dominick Street on the top floor of Hill's building, later Rooney's (now Tara) and it was there we were to stay for about four years. On the ground floor was

Fallon's radio and electrical shop and at the bottom of the stairs they had a large bust of Marconi, complete with bristling moustache. When I got old enough to annoy them they used to get rid of me by telling me that it was a bust of Hitler and even at that tender age I had heard of him and was rightly terrified. On the first floor below us lived the Coffey family. The father was a taxi man who had returned from the United States to escape the depression. He always sported a Yankee accent and a peaked cap with a button on the top. The children of this family, who were in or about the same age as I was, apart from a single son, were all absolutely beautiful girls, a fact that I noticed even at such a tender age. I played with them a lot.

Apart from the Coffey girls, my other passion was motoring and although there was but a handful of cars on the road in Galway in those war years I knew every one of them by sight, sound, and smell. Of course I had my own car, a tiny little grey pedal car with working headlights and an annoying little horn, which my dad bought for me almost as soon as I could sit in it. The main living area of our flat was large and spacious, and the floors were covered with linoleum, so I drove miles and miles around the furniture and under the table until my poor mother was nearly dizzy from watching me.

Dad got paid on Friday at around noon and for me this day was the highlight of the week, not because his humour always seemed to improve on Fridays, but because of the special lunch, or dinner as we called it then, that we always had on that day. At the top of Dominick Street in those days there was an Italian-owned fish and chip shop called The Lido, run by Mr and Mrs de Vito, famous for a collection of very beautiful daughters. This was good for business as all of the young Galway swains would go and have their fish suppers there just to sit and ogle the daughters. On his way home at Friday lunchtime my dad would stop off and get two large portions and one small portion of fish and chips, all wrapped in newspaper, and bring them home where my mother would have the plates warmed and the table set, salt and vinegar at the ready. I can still remember those dinners as if it were only a couple of weeks ago. There was something very special about the taste and smell of Italian-cooked fish and chips that was different from any other I have tasted since then.

Of course there were days too when the pay didn't quite stretch as far as it might have done and then we had what were known as 'tea dinners', usually something substantial enough but not very inviting. Still, Fridays were always different and always good. Around the corner from our flat, in lower Dominick Street, was a little bakery run by a lady working on her own called Miss Healy and she made wonderful heart-shaped queen cakes and apple and jam tarts. These too were an added treat for us at the weekends and I can still remember licking the warm strawberry jam off my chin.

The only oven we had in the flat was a patent device about twice the size of a biscuit tin, which sat atop our Primus stove and did its job very well. The only time that it wasn't up to the job was at Christmas time when my mother would go to great pains to get the Christmas cakes just exactly right. She was a great cook having learned from her mother and practised quite a bit as a cook in the family hotel, however the primus oven had a large hole at the bottom of it to allow the heat to enter and, if anything at all caused a puff of wind, the fruit would collapse, ruining the cake. My father and I didn't mind if the fruit collapsed but my mother was a perfectionist and would go and make another cake if the first one fell. As a result of this we would sometimes be found, when she wasn't looking, stamping about and banging doors so that the cake would collapse and we would have it before Christmas. We were never caught at this behaviour and didn't admit this until many years later.

In summer trips to the beach were *de rigueur* and we could walk with ease through Claddagh as far as Grattan Road which had a large, safe beach that sloped gently, allowing us to wade out for ages without fear of going over our depth. In those days only dads worked as a rule so the beach was quite a social place for all the mothers who could sit and talk to their friends and neighbours while keeping an eye on their various offspring building sandcastles and splashing about at the water's edge. Sandwiches and drinks were brought along and, since the beach was free, it was an inexpensive place to relax and enjoy life. Occasionally, if we went as far as Salthill itself, there was the possibility of actually getting an ice cream but these were very rare occasions indeed, especially since almost anything you could think of was rationed during the war years and could only be had by producing coupons.

Two major events during the war brought us back to the same beach to see great ships in the ship roads and also down to the docks. My father brought me in September 1939 to see the liner tender *Cathair na Gaillimhe* arrive to land the 430 survivors of the liner *Athenia* which it had transferred from the Norwegian tanker *Knute Nelson* at sea near the Aran islands. The *Athenia* was torpedoed at sea with some 1,400 passengers bound for Montreal in one of the first major acts of the ocean war. The whole town turned out to give any assistance it could and to show support for these unfortunate people.

In November 1940 just before my fifth birthday he brought me to see the huge Japanese liner which called to Galway to collect returning Japanese civilians who had made their way to neutral Ireland from all over Europe in order to be repatriated to their homeland. I have particular memories of this ship as it seemed to me to be as big as a town. Called *Husimi Maru*, it weighed some 11,000 tons and, in my memory, it was painted grey with sides so high they seem to go up forever.

Other events during the war were to have some effect on us as well. I remember when floating mines would stray into the bay; they would have to be disposed of by the Army. Their preferred method was to shoot from a good distance at the explosive vanes that stuck out of them like bristles, thereby exploding them with a tremendous bang that would shake the city, providing the barracks with a plentiful supply of fish as well. Before these events took place there was a car with a hand-operated siren on it, which would drive about warning people to open their windows to prevent their being broken by the explosion. For a small boy these were very exciting times indeed. Another night a Stirling bomber of the R.A.F. missed its course from the North of Ireland and ended up circling the city with one engine blazing as the crew baled out one by one. People rushed out when they heard the sound, but all they could see was the flaming glow in the sky from the engine. The pilot, fearful of the plane crashing on the city with its full load of bombs, ditched it in the sea off the lighthouse losing his life in the process but saving many in Galway from certain death.

At this time my father was often called out, sometimes at night, when various aircraft or parachutes or other devices, including stray barrage balloons, became entangled in, or damaged in some way, the electricity lines in the Galway district. Sometimes they were amongst the first on the scene and their finds were often gruesome. Perhaps the worst of these occurred when finding the crashed remains of an allied bomber near Gort in South Galway in which the entire crew was killed. This gave my father bad dreams for a long time afterwards.

3. *Learning to Fly*

—⚹—

Across the alleyway from our apartment was the Atlanta Hotel, an old-established family hotel, run by the very well-known Galway man, Josie Owens, a founder member of Corinithians Rugby Football Club in 1932, and also of the Galway Rovers Soccer Club, winner of many caps for Connacht and even for Ireland in 1936/37 in his rugby career. He was also a swimmer of some note, as well as an oarsman and cox. He went on in later years to become a very prominent local politician and was mayor of Galway in 1953/54.

One day there was knock on our apartment front door and, to my mother's astonishment, there was Josie with his finger up to his lips admonishing her to be quiet. He whispered to her not to move a muscle and silently and swiftly he moved past her into the living room and over to the bedroom door, which he opened quietly. My mother, not having a clue what was happening, stood her ground and resisted the urge to follow and see what he was up to. Suddenly he re-emerged with me in his arms, explaining to her that he was afraid she would make a noise and frighten me as I stood out on the windowsill three floors up looking around me as if I was out for a walk. He had seen me from a room in the hotel and dashed across the alleyway and up two flights of stairs. He had gone into the room without a sound and put his arm around my waist in a flash, whisking me to safety. At this time I was about three. My poor mother, when she realised how near I had come to disaster, nearly collapsed with shock, but Josie quickly made her some tea and she recovered in a couple of minutes. That evening when my father came home she told him the tale and from then until we left that apartment a couple of years later all of the windows were screwed shut at the bottom, and could only be opened at the top.

The following year it was time for me to start school and so I began the daily walk as far as the Presentation convent, a distance of about half a mile. The fact that the Coffey girls walked along with us made it easier and we could all play together at break time, so the whole thing wasn't as strange or as intimidating as it might have been. Sister Theresa was our first teacher and she was a gentle soul. A large open fire heated the classrooms in those days and, to keep our milk from being cold at lunchtime, Sister T decided to put our milk bottles standing along the mantelpiece. Of course they heated up and as one they all popped their corks or burst open spilling their contents about half an hour before lunchtime. There was much consternation cleaning up the mess and poor Sister T had to rush about and find enough milk for about thirty of us. She never put our bottles up to warm again no matter what the weather was like. I was to stay at that school on and off for the next four years.

The reason I say on and off is that sometime about 1941, my mother was suddenly taken ill with what was diagnosed at the time as pleurisy and confined to bed for several months. My father, unable to look after me and work at the same time, brought me down to Westport to be looked after by my aunt Gracie and my maternal grandparents. This was no hardship for me at all and I just loved living in Westport, as I got on great with my two cousins Thelma and Suzanne. Of course I had to be enrolled in school now that I had started, and so I went to the Presentation convent in Station Road, while my cousins went to the parish school run by Miss

Henderson for young Protestant children, the same school which my own mother had attended.

Used to being an only child, life in Westport was much more fun for me. I was now a member of an extended family group for the first time (with grandparents, an uncle, aunt and cousins) and I delighted in the whole business of being part of a large family. The house in Westport was a rambling old Georgian house on the Mall, which is by far the nicest part of the town. It had an enormous yard with stables that had been used to house the mail coach and the horses, and a huge back garden.

It was known as the Star Hotel (now the Boulevard) and operated as a small residential hotel that catered for commercial travellers and people who had to stay for short or even long terms in Westport. In contrast to our home in Galway, there were people everywhere in this house, aside from the family there were maids who helped with the cooking, doing the linen, making the beds and all the stuff that went on in a family hotel. There were a few long-term residents as well who were semi-permanent and to us were like part of the family.

The large kitchen was the hub of the house and my grandmother reigned supreme over this area. Large pots seemed to be always steaming or boiling and bread was being made from morning to night. There were soups and main courses to be prepared and the smell of roast beef or Irish stew or fresh bread assailed the senses like some wonderful perfume of life. In my memory I can still recall it from time to time, especially when cooking something that will set off a long forgotten olfactory nerve.

My grandmother, born Harriet Clarke, had come from Kilchreest near Loughrea in County Galway, where her father had been an R.I.C. policeman. He was only 45 when he died and his wife decided to marry again. In those days it was considered unacceptable and even improper to have single, unmarried girls in the same house as a stepfather, so Harriet and her sister, who were in their late teens by then, were sent away. Harriet was sent to live with and be a companion to a distant well-to-do female relation in Westport, while her sister Millicent immigrated to Australia where she became a schoolteacher. Before their parting they had an official photograph taken all dressed in their finery, so that each could remember the other. They never saw each other again and I still feel sad for them every time I look at this photograph. Shortly after Harriet's arrival in Westport she met up with my dashing grandfather and within a year or so they were married.

My maternal grandfather, Johnny Clampett, could not have been more different to my other Granda. He was tall and rangy, over six foot two, with a thin smiling face, and a large drooping moustache with waxed ends. He had poor eyesight by the time I knew him and he tended to squint when looking at you as if looking into bright sunlight. He always wore what to me looked like cowboy clothes. A wide-brimmed hat topped him off with a tweed or frieze split tail coat over narrow trousers, or britches which were completed with black polished knee length leggings, and black boots. He walked with that slight stoop that tall men sometimes affect and everywhere he went a couple of Jack Russell terriers snapped and danced about his heels. He chewed tobacco all the time and the bottom of his moustache was always dyed brown. He could have hit a fly, so accurate was his tobacco spit, and my grandmother was forever giving out to him and complaining about this nasty habit. He would wink at me behind her back when she was giving him one of these lectures and I always had to suppress a laugh when he did so, for my grandma could be pretty formidable when aroused.

He had spent his early life working with horses, stabling and driving them and for many years, before motorisation, he had held the mail contract to deliver the mail by coach from Westport to Louisburgh, a distance of 14 miles and back every day. He used to tell me that on good days he could do it twenty five minutes or half an hour and of course I believed him, but having driven the road many, many times since then I realise that it is hardly possible to do that in a modern car let alone in a four-wheeled coach behind two horses.

To assist with the supply of food for the hotel there was a vegetable garden complete with a coop full of hens out the back and he kept a couple of Jersey cows, always called Daisy and Diana, on a few acres that he had opposite the Westport Railway Station, now the site of an industrial estate. Every morning he had to go up to milk these cows and, if I had no school, I would be allowed to go along for the ride but was not allowed to assist with the milking.

Sometimes we went down to the farmyard at Westport House, where a friend of his, a Mr Gordon, was the manager. Westport House, the seat of Lord Sligo had an enormous herd of cows, and the farm had the first ever Alfa Laval milking machine I had ever seen, which could milk several cows at the same time. On these occasions I was allowed to turn the handle of milk separator in the large immaculate dairy. Turning the handle gave off a humming sound not unlike the droning of a distant airplane and this appealed to me no end. Needless to mention I was probably giving the dairymaid a break, or else I was in her way, but either way she was polite enough not to complain and I would happily twist away while my young muscles would last. Although the thought of it makes me shudder now, sometimes as a reward I was given a drink of the fresh cream. Think of the cholesterol!

At home in the hotel there was no separating machine so we left the milk overnight in earthenware crocks with sterilised muslin draped through it to separate the cream. In the morning my grandmother or one of the maids would slowly lift off the muslin taking the cream with it and depositing it into a special crock for this purpose. The skimmed milk was then fed to the calves when there were any, and the muslins were boiled and prepared for the following day.

The house was a musical house and whenever there was any leisure time somebody, usually my Aunt Gracie, would begin belting out songs on the piano and we would all join in and sing. Favourites of the time were the old Victorian music hall songs such as *Show Me the Way to Go Home,* and *My Old Man Said Follow the Band,* as well as many of Tom Moore's melodies. My cousins Thelma and Suzanne and I were expected to perform when asked, so we learned at an early age to stand up and sing when requested. My Uncle Arthur, who also worked for the E.S.B., played the ukulele and the mandolin so we were never short of a robust accompaniment.

Family concerts were the order of the day, and on Sunday evenings there was often a singsong, in which the patrons of the hotel also sang along.

Saturday afternoon was the time my grandfather went hunting. He had permission from Lord Sligo, with whom he was on friendly terms, to hunt for rabbits over the demesne, so along with a pack of Jack Russell terriers and some of his cronies we would walk the land listening to the hullabaloo when the dogs took off, retrieving the rabbits that they managed to kill. As a result of this of course roast or stewed rabbit was often on the menu.

There was also another family of Clampetts along the Mall and these were the family of Tom Clampett, my grandfather's brother. He lived in a house called Malvern which had been the family home of their parents. Tom was married to a Scottish lady known to all as Aunt Mary, who had such a strong Scottish accent that in the beginning I had trouble understanding a word she was saying. She came from the Isle of Skye and they had one son Jack and one daughter Olive who was a contemporary of my mother and who by that time had a daughter Stephanie, another cousin with whom I played. The families, especially the younger ones, moved freely from house to house and so I often found myself sitting down to dinner in Malvern rather than in the hotel kitchen. Their kitchen too was a large room with an enormous table which could seat ten or twelve at a sitting if needed, and out the back there was a large garden which, like the hotel, was fully planted with all sorts of vegetables and potatoes, as well as fruit trees and bushes. I particularly enjoyed the loganberries, something you never or hardly ever see nowadays.

For my fourth birthday I was given a bicycle. It was a half-sized machine made by a company called Hopper, and it was blue. It had a carrier on the back and although initially I was too short to reach the pedals from the lowest setting of the saddle, I could manage alright while sitting on the carrier, so for several weeks this is how I cycled about Westport and to and from school.

I could read at a very early age, and my special treat every week was to go to McGreevy's newsagents and pick up a copy of the

Beano and the *Dandy*. By the time I was able to saddle the bike properly, I would clip these treasures carefully to the carrier and cycle home, where several entertaining hours would be spent savouring the comics. I loved Corky the Cat, Keyhole Kate and Lord Snooty and his pals, as well as desperate Dan and Pansy Potter the strongman's daughter.

Sometimes I would go fishing in the Mall River, where plenty of small trout were to be seen. I was not allowed to use a real hook, so a compromise was a bit of bread fixed to a safety pin. Needless to mention I never actually caught any fish but did manage to feed quite a few, while all the time dreaming of catching a really big one.

One of the almost permanent residents of the Star Hotel was a man called Alf McMahon, who was some sort of commercial traveller though I can't recall what company he represented. Because of his occupation and the remoteness of the areas he travelled he had an allocation of petrol, so for very special treats the entire family would pile into his car, which I seem to remember was a Morris Fourteen, and head for the beach at Old Head or Lecanvey, the seaside resorts outside Westport, and we would sing aloud all the way there and all the way back, usually rounds such as *Row, Row, Row Your Boat Gently Down the Stream,* and our all time favourite, *I've Got Sixpence Jolly, Jolly Sixpence.*

The other regular resident at the hotel was a small wizened little man called Gus Delahunt who was, as far as I can remember, an electrician but in a private capacity doing contract work and not working for the E.S.B. Gus, who always wore a hat inside or outside the house, always seemed to have a butt of a cigarette protruding for the corner of his mouth. Although he was a serious little man most of the time, he could make funny faces and funny noises with his mouth that sounded like a squealing cat. He would sometimes do this to annoy the girls working there but also to amuse us kids.

Together with my oldest cousin Thelma and her kid sister Suzanne, I would often hang around the town, calling in at various shops and places where we were known. We would call to Mars O'Donnell, who had been my mother's bridesmaid, on the Castlebar Street. Mars had a little sweet shop and when we would buy a pennyworth of sweets she would always put in a few extra. She also sold other exotica such as liquorice sticks or pipes, and sherbet bags, and our favourite thing of all, lucky bags, which would contain some sweets and a surprise. Around the corner from Mars's shop on the Mall her father had a shoemaker's shop. He was a deaf mute and we would watch in fascination as he and his assistant, who was also deaf, would carry on conversations in sign language, which sometimes ended in fierce arguments. We didn't know how to do it, but invented a sign language of our own which we would use to impress our friends. The sights and sounds of O'Donnell's shop were fascinating to a small boy. We were allowed to watch as they actually made shoes from the sole up and then stitched them and finally polished them. They made boots and some articles of harness as well as far as my memory recalls. There was also a particular smell to the place of cured leather and wax and polish and the memory of O'Donnell's often returns when I sit on a new leather sofa or pick up a new pair of shoes.

By far the greatest fright of my young life was when visiting the coffin makers next door to The Star Hotel. One day the young boys working there, as a joke, got me to go in one of the coffins and closed the lid. I didn't mind for a minute or two, thinking that they were just having a bit of fun, but when they didn't open for several minutes I began to panic and banged on the lid. Eventually they opened it and thought it was a huge joke. Their boss didn't think so and gave them a serious telling off. I was lucky not to have developed serious claustrophobia as a result. I didn't go in there for a long time afterwards and perhaps that may have been their idea in the first place.

Sometimes too I would hang out with some of the local lads from my school and we would wander about looking for some mischief. I remember a day when we decided to have snowball fights but not with snowballs as it was in the summer, but with balls of horse dung, which were very plentiful in the yard of a local flour mill where horses gathered and waited all day. When I got home that day I recall being stripped, given a few slaps on the bum and immersed in a large, hot bath until the smell had died down sufficiently for me to be allowed to associate with 'civilised' people again. I was discouraged from hanging out with that gang of boys again. No doubt, after a week or two had passed, we were up to some more mischief or other as if the warning had never been issued.

Beside the Town Hall there was another sweet shop belonging to a man called McHale and he had an ice cream machine which made those delicious whipped ice cream cones; it was a special treat to be brought for a walk as far as McHales and given one of his famous cones. It was my first introduction to whipped cream ices and I was addicted from the start.

All in all, I had very happy times in Westport, and when my mother joined us after her long confinement in bed I was even happier. Of course this was only a holiday for her for a week or two and then together we went back to Galway to a new apartment. Although I occasionally spent holidays there after that, the next long trip there was in 1947 during the famous blizzard.

I was about twelve years old when this great snow storm came and as luck would have it was visiting Westport. My father was called out in Galway to deal with broken power lines and all of the difficulties such a blizzard can cause. My mother and I found ourselves stranded in Westport as it was cut off for about five or six weeks from the outside world. My mother wasn't too pleased to be cut off from my dad but I was in my element. Having no school I spent weeks with the boys sliding down the mighty high Peter Street on makeshift toboggans made out of bent sheets of galvanised iron.

Eventually after some seven weeks we got to go home, only to find that all of the pipes in our house had frozen and as soon as we lit a fire the ice melted and the place was filled with water. It took my poor mother about a week to get the place back to normal.

4. Montpellier Terrace

—◊◊—

This was the rather grand name of our next address. I have no idea what connection the particular street had with the Southern French city, but we moved into number 3, which was a nineteenth century two storey house. It was a more up-market area than Dominick Street and most of the neighbours were pretty well to do, many of them in the legal or medical professions. We rented the two front floors from a Miss Molloy and she kept a separate little apartment for herself in the back portion of the house. There was a tiny front garden filled with nasturtiums and clematis and a large long back garden with an old mews stable building behind. My mother had by now recovered from her illness and in the front room or parlour she set up her piano.

It was at this time that she decided to go back to teaching piano, so she began to practice every spare hour that she had so that she might get her teaching qualification from the London College of Music, which was being operated by a Dr Lloyd-Weber, the father of the now famous Andrew and Julian. Morning, noon and night she practised and no matter where I went in the house I could hear it; arpeggios, eight octave scales and five-finger exercises went on endlessly. Chopin, Mozart and Rachmaninoff filled my every waking hour until she eventually sat and passed the exam and she became an A.L.C.M. (Associate of the London College of Music) (subsequently becoming an L.C.M. (Licentiate of the London College) and then an F.L.C.M. (Fellow etc.) and in the early 1980s was elected as the first full Member of the London College of Music in Ireland and was honoured at a special reception in London.

Armed with her diploma she began then to teach the piano. My father, very proud of her achievement, bought her a brass plate that he fixed to the front door. It read, rather grandly, Jeanne M. Byrne A.L.C.M. Pianoforte Tuition. Now the sound in the house went from her own accomplished playing to the halting inharmonious stumbling of beginners. It was nearly more than any child could take, so I took myself off at every opportunity to escape the apparently incessant hammering of the piano.

It is a habit of only children to join themselves on to larger families for companionship and fun and such a family were the O'Sullivans who lived around the corner from us in Devon Place. Mr O'Sullivan, Bartley, had a job with the Department of Lands and he and his wife had two sons and three daughters. One of the sons and one of the daughters were about my age, so I adopted them. Tom later told me that his first encounter with me was on the beach when I came up and asked, "Can I play with you?" This apparently cemented our relationship, since I spent much of my free time for the next several years as a supernumerary to the O'Sullivan family.

One of their favourite leisure pastimes as a family on Sunday afternoons was to go down to The Corrib Rowing and Yachting Club, of which they were members, and take out a couple of randans (light rowing boats) and row en famille up as far as Menlo Castle or even Menlo Graveyard and picnic there complete with a fire made up from driftwood, which we had to gather, and tea made in a kettle which they boiled on the fire. This tea had a special flavour that is hard to replicate. For me this was a new paradise as my father, as a consequence of having been thrown in the docks in a rough and tumble with his mates when he was about twelve and narrowly escaping being drowned, was afraid of boats and water and wouldn't ever go near them.

Bartley O'Sullivan was involved with the setting up or the operation of the Conamara Pony Show in Clifden. I don't know if this was as a consequence of his job with the department or whether it was a personal hobby. One way or another every year in August we would all pile in his car which was a large Austin and head out to Clifden for the show. Again this was an occasion for a picnic and we could watch the ponies as they paraded and went through their paces and generally have a great time helping out. The O'Sullivan's eldest son Tadhg, was a student in University College Galway and also for a time an actor in An Taibhdhearc, the Irish language theatre, and we all paraded down to see him perform. I remember he and Sean McGlory (later to go to Hollywood and spend his life as an actor there) practising a sword fight with real rapiers in O'Sullivan's back yard. I was hugely impressed. Tadhg went on to join the Irish diplomatic corps and become an Irish ambassador to Nigeria, Moscow and Washington. The O'Sullivan family enriched my young life in so many ways that I have been indebted to them for most of my life.

I was still at this time going to the Presentation, but now had to take a different, longer route to school and used to have to start earlier. Along the way I would meet up with other scholars heading in the same direction, one of these, a delightful blonde who happened to be born on exactly the same day as myself, became my latest passion. Her name was Mary and we had to hold hands so as not to get lost or wander off on the way to school and this was just fine with me. I think she was probably the first girl I ever kissed, at about the tender age of six or seven and although I knew that it was something little boys weren't supposed to do or enjoy, I must confess that I liked it.

In those days birthdays were celebrated on the actual birthday itself and one of the disadvantages of being born on the same day was that neither of us ever could go to each other's parties. We did, however, send each other birthday cards and used to exchange cake the next day at school.

It was around this time that I had my first real fight. Down the road from us, near the Jesuit Church, was a group of small shops and I used to be sent for things like bread, butter or milk if we ran out at home. I would be given the money and, I presume, the coupon and given a note for the lady in the shop. Next door to one of these shops lived a family of tough guys, who were known to gang up on weaker kids and give them a hiding and steal their sweets and stuff like that.

One day as I was just reaching the shop the biggest of them, who was about a year or two older than me, came over and jostled me to the ground grabbing the money which had fallen from my hand in the affray, then they all ran off. I ran home crying to tell my mother and as luck would have it my grandfather was on one of his sporadic visits. "Great," I thought, "now he'll come down and beat them all up," but no, that was not what happened. He took me aside and gave me a little lecture. He told me that as I went through life I would meet up with many bullies, that bullies were really cowards and were no good at all without a gang to back them up. What I should do when next confronted was to stand up to them, let them see that I was not afraid of them and they would just crumble. He then gave me the sixpence or whatever money I had lost and told me to go back again and get the message I was sent for.

This was not the solution I had hoped for, but armed with the information my Granda had given me and with not a little trepidation, I started down again to the shop. When I was within yards of the shop door my tormentors appeared again, the big one to the fore. Again he gave me a shove and told me to hand over my dough, but this time I decided that I would have to stand up to him as my Granda would be waiting at home to know how I got on. I hardly aimed at all but took a very solid swing in the direction of his face, putting all my weight behind it and struck him fair and square on his nose, which began to pour blood. To my astonishment he began to bawl crying and he and his brother ran off, leaving me to go to the shop and get the messages. Forever after that when I met him he took good care to avoid confrontation and once even crossed the road to get away from me. My grandfather was very proud, not so much that I had bloodied his nose but that I had stood up for myself. Within a week he had given me a book entitled *Boxing for Boys*.

I suppose that at this time I was around six and a half to seven years old and I had broadened my area of operations and ventured as far as Fr. Griffin Road and Munster Avenue, although in those days I seem to recall it was called Munster Lane. Many of my friends lived over that side of the neighbourhood and we played football and wrestling and rough and tumble in the fields behind O'Flaherty's garage. It was great place and at a drop of a hat could become the Wild West when we were playing cowboys or even the wild ocean if we were being pirates. Among my friends there were the McInerney family who had two boys Enda and Kieran, in or about my own age. I was very pally with them and we got up to all sorts of mischief. Their father was a foreman in Curley's garage in Prospect Hill and as a result he had a car, which was quite a rare thing in those days. We used to go and sit in the car, pretending to be driving it and the boys were even allowed to start it up, or so they said.

One of the differences between the Mac brothers and myself was that they were allowed to stay out for a while at night, while for me this was always forbidden. My parents were very fond of the pictures, or the flicks as my father called them, and a couple of nights a week, especially at the weekends they would go to the Estoria which was, literally, just around the corner. One day I hatched the brave plot that if I could get out when they were gone, I could go over and hang out with the McInerney boys and I knew they would be impressed. So on the next night that they were heading out I was sent to bed as usual before they left and Miss Molloy given the nod that I was safely out of harm's way.

Miss Molloy had agreed that she would keep and eye and ear out for me, while they were gone, as she herself was not one for the films, preferring instead to listen to the radio in the evenings. After about a quarter of an hour, I slipped out of bed and dressed myself, crept down the stairs, past Miss Molloy's door, made sure that the key was on the string inside the letterbox and slipped quietly out into the night. Of course it was summer time and still as bright as day, but it was after half past eight and that was an hour and a half after my bedtime. I went over to Mac's and hung out with the boys and slipped back in about an hour later and nobody was the wiser. Or so I thought; but my mother met Mrs McInerney the next day and she mentioned in passing that I had been out playing with the lads in their front garden the night before. When my father got home from work that evening all hell broke loose and my behind stung with the trace of his belt for a long time. To say that I was grounded for the rest of my young life was an understatement. Miss Molloy was mortified and the key was never left on a string again. Instead my parents had keys of their own and so had Miss Molloy and when the door was locked at night that was it; it was definitely locked.

Around about this time my mother decided that it was now time for me to learn to play the piano. There was to be no more dodging. At this time in my life I did not like the piano at all and in fact it might be truer to say that I really hated it. Nevertheless the torture began. The slow, laborious scales that had so blighted my life were now emanating from my own stumbling fingertips as I sat reluctantly at the piano. I could play them but I didn't want to. There could be no question of this; what would people say if the music teacher couldn't teach her own son to play the piano. It was unthinkable. What made it worse of course was the fact that I had to be taught in front of other pupils waiting their turn and my mother would say things like, "You could play that much better Nora couldn't you?" and poor Nora or whoever would have to nod in agreement or just blush with embarrassment. This used to mortify me and for a while I made a valiant effort and even learned to play a few tunes. I could read music fairly well, but hated the business of sitting in front of the dreaded piano, with my mother watching over my shoulder waiting for me to make a mistake so that she could launch another lecture at me. Eventually of course it became a battle of wills and although I did go on to sit and pass a few exams, my dislike continued unabated.

Somebody then suggested that it was very difficult for her to attempt to teach her own offspring and that she might get better results if I were to go to another teacher. As bad luck would have it, only three doors away from our house in number 6 there were not just one, but two other music teachers. The Misses Fahy were small birdlike Victorian ladies, both of whom taught music in the two magnificent front living rooms of their house. They were the epitome of what one expects a music teacher to be, genteel and slightly arty. I was destined for Cissy who was better able to handle the hard cases than her sister. Of course my mother had briefed her on all of my foibles and told her to take no nonsense and so any stubbornness on my part was met with a sharp crack across the knuckles with an old ivory ruler. This had the effect of hardening my resolve and after about two terms, my mother was advised that whatever I was to learn, she should forget the idea of me as a pianist. Eventually I was spared, but this was some years later, when my mother, who tried every ploy from bribery to dire threats, finally admitted defeat and gave up on me.

By now I was in first class in the Presentation School, which was as high as boys could go. I was in the hands of a lay teacher now, a dear kind woman called Bean Uí Dhuigneáin, not to be confused with her sister-in-law who was also a dear kind woman of the same name who taught in Scoil Fhursa, the Irish school. Mrs Duignan was very taken by the fact that I could stand up and sing a song, almost any song, when asked and began to ask me to perform from time to time. Now I didn't mind doing this for our own class who were used to me and me to them, but when she took to sending me up to the senior classes to perform in front of older girls, especially in the secondary school I was mortified. Fortunately it didn't last too long, for the next year was to be one of the biggest changes in my young life. I was heading for the Bish and we were changing house yet again: this time for good and to a whole house of our own.

5. Devon Park

—⁓—

Our next move was to Devon Park in Lower Salthill although, no more than Montpellier Terrace, I have no idea what possible connection there might have between this area and Devon in England. Perhaps it was somebody's idea of giving the place a bit of class, comparing it with the garden of England. What it was, however, was a pretty, nice, little development of around twenty-five or so houses, many of which were built by the Galway Corporation as a slightly more up-market housing estate, aimed at blue collar workers who could afford to pay the rent. Eventually the tenants would be allowed to buy these houses out altogether. My dad was lucky to be accepted for one of the houses and so we proudly moved our furniture even further away from the city, to what was then really a garden suburb of Galway.

This was an entire three-bedroom terrace house, with a sitting room complete with bay window, a large kitchen and a scullery or pantry. Upstairs were three bedrooms, a bathroom and separate toilet. Although I had always had a room to myself, this was a real decent sized room that I could put my own stamp on, with plenty of room to store all my toys and gear. Behind the house was a small garden about thirty feet by forty feet with a five-foot high concrete wall surrounding the lot. Behind the garden was heaven in the shape of acres and acres of unbroken fields that stretched for more than a mile, but more about that later.

Although the estate had been built for about five or six years at this stage, the roads had not yet been surfaced, so the whole place resembled a country lane, complete with puddles and mud when it rained. The main entrance to the entire estate area was a rather crude breach in the eight feet high stone wall that had once been part of the estate walls of Lenaboy House, once home of the O'Hara Burke family but now a girl's orphanage. About fifty metres north of this was a cross roads with about ten houses to the right and twelve or so on our side to the left. At the head of our road was a large builder's shed made from galvanised corrugated iron. This shed had been used as an office and store by the builder of the fancier one-off detached houses further up the road on the way to Taylor's Hill, which the folks there rather grandly called Lenaboy Taylor's Hill. These houses were designed and built for people whose positions in life meant that they could aspire to such luxury. The name of the builder of these houses was Gleeson and the shed was always known as Gleeson's shed or just the shed, which is how I will mention it.

Along the southern side of this shed was an exposed concrete foundation, which protruded about two feet from the face of the building and was about eighteen inches high. It could hold about ten or twelve sitting in comparative comfort. This is where the gang used to hang out. When I arrived they were sitting there, checking us out. Young and old kids sat there and those that couldn't get a seat on the concrete sprawled on the grass in front of it. This was the first time apart from a schoolyard that I had met a gang and I had to approach them warily. Fortunately our next door neighbour Steve O'Brien, who was around the same age as myself had been there for longer than us and after introducing myself to him, he introduced me to the gang and in no time at all I too had my bum on the seat at Gleeson's shed.

For the next ten years or more this was to be our forum, theatre, office and headquarters. Whenever you left the house you shouted back, "I'll be up at the shed" and your parents knew that you were safe and easily reachable if they wanted you. Nothing came in or out of Devon Park without passing that shed and almost always there was some sentry on duty to pass on the word. Behind the seat was an old green wooden door and everyone past and present carved their initials on it and so it resembled the famous autograph tree in Coole Park and carried hundreds of carved autographs. I often felt that it should have been preserved as a piece of local folk heritage when the shed was finally demolished in the late fifties.

Not far from the shed was Aylward's dump. It belonged to Aylward's garage whose owner Mick Aylward lived in Devon Park. This was a graveyard for old motorcars and their component parts and for a young car fanatic like me it was heaven. During the war there were very few private cars on the road because of the shortage of petrol and it was not uncommon for car owners to ask their local garage to store them for them until they could put them back on the road. In this way there was a good mix of interesting cars some parked outside Aylward's house, some in the large shed at the back of their house and even some on the road into the dump itself. They were mostly Vauxhalls or Opels as Aylward was the General Motors dealer and garage, but there were a few pieces of exotica such as M.G. tourers and Riley Nines. Within weeks of arriving there I knew all of these cars inside and out and, as many of them were not locked, if you were wary you could spend many a happy hour driving around the world in your imagination. Sometimes old Aylward or his more ferocious foreman Larry Craughwell would stage a raid and we'd have to leg it over the fields to escape. In retrospect I suppose that we were a great nuisance to these men, but we felt that since nobody was using these cars they were fair game. It is fair to say though that in all the time we hung out there, apart from wearing their batteries out, I can't remember anybody doing any real damage to the cars, not like today I fear, when they would certainly be vandalised beyond recognition in no time at all.

In fine weather (and my memory makes it seem as if it were always fine in those days) we spent our days and our evenings 'up the fields'. The fields in question were the remains of the O'Hara Burke Lenaboy Estate and they stretched from our back garden as far as Threadneedle Road with not a house in between except for Dalysfort House. The fields belonged to two orders of nuns, those nearest our house belonged to the Mercy sisters who ran Lenaboy House as St Anne's orphanage and girls' school, while those further away belonged to the Dominican sisters from Taylor's Hill convent and school. There was no restriction however to our using them and use them we did.

About a hundred yards or so from our back wall was the remains of the drive or avenue to Lenaboy house and this was a wide flat field bordered on one side by a fine stand of beech trees and another by a gently rising slope that made a perfect seating area. About one hundred yards long and something less that forty wide, this was known as 'the pitch' and it was there that every known game under the sun was played. Gaelic football and hurling were every-day events in season, while soccer and even rugby were also played there but not with the same regularity. In a smaller flat field closer to the road we played rounders in summer and this of course ended up being called the rounders pitch.

Rounders, which is a bit like baseball, was one of the favourite games for summertime as everybody could play whether boys or girls, young or old and teams could be a small or as large as required on the day. When the Galway races came around, some of us became horses and others became jockeys and jumps were raised from furze bushes around the perimeter of the pitch and we ran our own Galway races over and over again.

The Gleeson kids were part of our gang and their uncle had a real racehorse. This horse was called Carrantráile after the area from which they originated I think, and another Galway horse that actually won the Galway Hurdle was Fair Pearl, the mount of Mickey Tully. Everybody wanted to be one of these two horses, as they were the only two horses whose names we actually knew. Other names would be made up on the day; things like Devon Flyer, or Salthill Sport were the order of the day. The horse was usually the bigger of the two in our case, with a rope reins that passed behind the nape his neck and around under his shoulders leaving two tails with which he might be steered by the jockey.

The races were fiercely competed for and the ability to jump the jumps and run fast was a much sought after quality in both the horse and jockey. Sean Burke was the fastest thing on two legs and he was always in great demand as either a horse or a jockey. In the autumn when the Dublin horse show was on, this whole game slowed down a bit and the jumps got higher and lo and behold we were the horse show. Long summer days passed very pleasantly in these pursuits.

When we were 'up the fields' nobody would dream of going home until they were called and various families had their own distinctive call signs with which they summoned their young. My father had a shrill whistle, which was achieved by putting thumb and first finger together into the mouth and blowing with all his might; this sound would carry great distances and I never had an excuse for being late. The Sheridan family had a large brass bell, which was rung in their back yard. The Ryan girls' father had a police whistle, the Quigley's father clapped his hands in their front porch, which had a sort of acoustic that amplified it. Others had referees' whistles and little secret whistles that were recognisable to their own offspring.

Once while I was climbing a large beech tree, my father whistled just as I was near the top and so I rushed to get down and slipped, a piece of a broken branch went up the leg of my short trousers and came out at the top, suspending me some fifteen or sixteen feet above the ground. Since it was behind my back I could do nothing to free myself and I just hung there in space. All of my friends had gone home at this stage to their lunches and I could hear my father getting closer and madder thinking that I was ignoring his whistle and causing him to waste valuable time from his lunch hour. When he got within hailing distance he heard me shouting and nearly had a heart attack on the spot when he saw my predicament. Not being a tree climber himself he was helpless to assist me, but seeing that I was reasonably safe, provided my trousers didn't burst, he went looking for help. He rounded up a couple of the bigger lads who could climb and I was eventually lifted high enough between them to disengage my trousers and scramble free. Of course my father was relieved that I was safe, but that did not stop him from giving me a cuff in the ear for wasting his entire lunch break. My mother also was less than pleased as the lunch which had literally been on the table when I was called had to be returned to the oven to keep it warm and was by now reduced to a crisper, dryer version of the original. Nobody seemed to care that I didn't do it on purpose. Still the argument was that I shouldn't be climbing trees in the first place and furthermore certainly shouldn't be climbing them when there was nobody else around to assist if I got into difficulties. It was a long time before I went solo tree climbing again.

One day a few of us were hanging out at the entrance to Devon Park, which we sometimes did during the summer months to see the world go by. The bus stopped across the road from us and out got two genuine real-live, fully uniformed American soldiers. Now the only American soldiers we had ever seen before this were in the pictures but suddenly here they were on our street with their best uniforms on and their kit bags thrown over their shoulders. We were fully aware of how to speak to American soldiers so we went across to them and asked them, in the manner of street urchins all over the world, "Got any gum, chum?" They laughed and of course pulled out packets of gum from their pockets, which they gave us willingly. The only problem was that none of us had ever actually seen chewing gum before except in the pictures and while we got the idea of eating it and chewing it for a while most of us swallowed it too. The two soldiers were on leave from the European war theatre, which was almost over at this stage, and since one of them had a Galway ancestor decided to have a look around the place. They asked us if we knew of any guest houses as they didn't want to stay in fancy hotels. The only one fully open at this time of the year, which was very early summer, was Foy's guest house in Lenaboy Avenue and so we proudly led them along the road, like two prize trophies. As soon as they were installed in Foy's they said they would like us to show them around the next day and of course we were as proud as could be.

Although these soldiers were probably only privates, their uniforms had more stripes and badges than we had ever seen before. On their chests they had twenty or more medal ribbons of every colour under the sun; more than one would expect to see on a picture of General de Gaulle. For the next couple of days we saw them around and took them on a walkabout of the parts of Galway we knew. They gave us lots of chewing gum, which by now we knew how to use, and little packets of sweets called Life Savers. Since sweets were in very short supply in Ireland at the time, we guarded these with miserly restraint. Eventually it came time for them to leave and we bade them almost tearful farewells before they boarded the bus that would start them back on their journey to Europe. They gave every one of us a medal ribbon, which we cherished for years afterwards. This had been our first real encounter with real, live American soldiers.

Thirty two years later I was telling this story to a group of American academics during the course of a lecture on Irish theatre which I was giving in Stonehill College in Boston to the American Committee of Irish Studies. After the lecture one of the professors came up to me and said, "You're not going to believe this, but I was one of those two soldiers and after we went back to Europe, my buddy went one way and I went another and we never met again." The following day by way of proof he brought me copies of several letters which he had received from Mrs Foy, the landlady with whom we had placed him and with whom he struck up a great friendship over the years until her death a few years previously.

In summer no day would be complete without at least one swim. An hour after our lunches, for nobody was allowed to swim until an hour after eating, we would assemble en masse at the shed with our swimming trunks, or togs as we called them then, rolled in a towel under the arm and when sufficient numbers had assembled off we headed for Salthill. We took the short cut across the fields, up across the pitch around the edges of the nun's meadow across a couple of stone walls and down Dalysfort road. We were a rag tag bunch ranging in age from about six or seven up to thirteen or fourteen and every one of us could swim. Not only that, but we were strong swimmers and we spent hours in and out of the sea.

Swimming was segregated in those more puritanical days. This meant that there was a ladies swimming area at the Promenade that had a beach as well as diving boards and the men had their own place at Blackrock that was deeper and had no beach. One presumes now that the reason was to keep the sexes from being an 'occasion of sin' to one another. We, being kids, could get away with swimming in the women's area, which was much more popular and also more fun. Sometimes if we had a really hot summer we would go for a swim in the morning and another in the afternoon and just laze about on the beach soaking up the summer sun. Of course we were unaware of the risk of skin cancer and stuff like that then and most of us were tanned like old leather by about July. If we got burned it was calamine lotion that was rubbed in. Strangely enough one of the counter measures to sunburn in those days was to rub olive oil on the skin before sunbathing. This to me always seemed to make the sun burn hotter, but what did I know? Who was I to interfere with tradition? In later years Nivea cream was substituted for olive oil. At least this smelt better though I'm not sure what sun repellent properties it had.

In the summer evenings some parents would sometimes come out and sit or hang out with the kids around the rounders pitch and from time to time even join in on other occasions. Sometimes jokes would be told and impromptu concerts would be held. Anybody who could perform at any level was expected to do so. This could take any form, from singing to whistling or performing on the tin whistle or the mouthorgan. A surprising number of kids and adults in this neighbourhood were fine singers and performers on various makeshift instruments and these concerts were always a success. At times like this Devon Park was a happy place to live for children and parents alike. I'm sure there were troubled times for all as well, what with the country in a serious recession most of the time and people losing their jobs and other fathers having to emigrate to England to feed their families, but somehow or other to us kids, summer always seemed to be a happy time.

6. Games

—⁓—

Games were played by all and seemed to be seasonal. Girls were always skipping ropes up around the shed no matter what time of the year it was and sometimes some of the lads would join in, when there was nothing else happening, and they would call out mantra-like chants.

> *Teddy bear teddy bear turn around*
> *Teddy bear teddy bear touch the ground*
> *Teddy bear teddy bear show me your shoe*
> *Teddy bear teddy bear that will do.*

This was an example that comes to mind and it would be chanted as they were skipping and the skipper was expected to perform the task called out to them while not losing a beat. Other games were played with a ball against the shed door and other chants would be called as the ball player had to change hands or turn around completely or touch the ground, or catch the ball under their knee. Skipping and ball games would be played at any time of the year, all the time, while other games came and went with the seasons.

Wallflowers, wallflowers growing up so high,
All pretty children who do not want to die,
Except Julia Murphy is the only one,
Oh piper shin O piper shin
Turn your back to the wall again.

The girls used to chant this as they danced about in a ring holding hands. She whose name was called out had to turn her back and continue to go around in a circle, though for her it was now going backwards which made it more difficult. They continued in this manner until all or most of them were turned around, causing the ring to become unstable and collapse. (I quote the words phonetically in the above from memory and have no idea who or what piper shin is).

Then there was Hop Scotch, which required several numbered squares to be drawn on the ground in a particular manner and was negotiated by hopping sometimes on one leg and others on two around the course as dictated by the numbers. All of these games were very physical and as a result there were no fat or obese children in our day.

There was a season for Conkers or Chestnuts, which was usually about the middle of October when the best chestnuts would be found on Cloherty's tree at Nile lodge. Sticks would have to be thrown up to dislodge the chestnuts because once the season started we couldn't be bothered to wait for them to fall naturally. This gave rise to near misses with Cloherty's windows and occasionally quick retreats when, in exasperation, their two Scots Terriers, Boots and Candy, would be released. They chased as a team and were pretty formidable at the pincer movement; one of them came out of one gate and the other came out the second gate and you were caught between them.

The freshest chestnuts were no good for conkers as they were soft and broke easily, but 'seasoners' sequestered from the previous year and dried in the airing cupboard were as hard as rocks and could easily become conquerors (Conkers). The best one I ever had was a two-year seasoner that I bought for two pence and was a conqueror fifty.

Of course there were tricksters in this game too, some who would fill the shell of the chestnut with lead and other, slight-of-hand merchants who would have a seasoner on one end of the string, which they would hold when it was their turn to be hit and a large iron nut on the other end of the string which they would use when it was their turn to hit. Such guys had to be avoided at all costs and if you were in doubt it was prudent to ask to see both ends of the string before engaging.

Another favourite pastime in season was playing marbles, although many of the marbles available during the war were pretty basic things called crockers, as they were made not from glass but a rather poor quality of crockery. There were also some glass ones available and these were highly prized, sometimes valued at twice or three times the value of a crocker. There were two basic games; one was played along the street gutters, in which you rolled off your marble and your opponent tried to reach and touch it with his own, or get within a hand span of it. If he failed then you had the opportunity to touch his and so on until one hit the other and the one who did the hitting was the winner, claiming the other's marble as his prize. The other game was a more sophisticated version in which each member put a single marble into a circle and then took turns at knocking them out. Any marble you knocked out you could keep but if your marble stayed in the circle you had to leave it there. They both sound to be pretty basic games but they occupied us for days on end during the marble season. We were easily amused back in those simple days.

Being the war years, the roads were empty except for the G.S.R. (Great Southern Railway) buses, which plied between Eyre Square and Salthill, and the large ten-wheeled Ford trucks that went back and forth all day carrying turf from the bogs of Conamara to the green in Eyre Square. The turf was stacked under armed guard for use as a fuel on the Galway to Dublin trains, as there was no coal available during these years.

One of the games we played was with our spinning tops along

the road from where we lived out to the top of the Promenade in Salthill. The one who got there and back in the least number of lashes of the whip was the winner. For those of you who have never seen tops, they were a piece of turned wood about two and a half inches high, tapering from about an inch and a half in diameter to nothing with a metal point at the bottom. They were coloured in different shades for identification purposes and when you got them going by spinning them with the string of your whip, you chased after them and lashed them while they were still turning, thereby driving them a further distance along the road, whereupon you ran after them and lashed them again and so on. While it may seem a pointless exercise, it required a certain amount of skill to do it right and was probably no more pointless to our minds than golf is to those who follow it today. There were smaller, lighter tops too called racing tops, and they were T-shaped and travelled farther and quicker when struck.

Roller skates too had their season, but they were crude heavy metal objects compared with those one sees today. They fitted on to your shoe with a sort of clamp. If your shoes were old, as they often were, you ran the risk of having the soles pulled off completely. A strap went over the instep and the better ones had wheels that turned on ball bearings. Cheaper models had to be greased and could seize if improperly maintained.

I remember frightening myself to death on one occasion when in search of a thrill, I held on to the luggage ladder at the back of the bus, thinking that it would stop in a hundred yards or so – in those days the buses stopped wherever you put up your hand to hail them as there were no official stops. Needless to mention I was wrong and the bus continued for about half a mile or more at about twenty or twenty five miles an hour with me hanging on to the ladder behind for dear life. I never did that again.

In winter there would be snow from time to time, although it didn't last long generally because of our proximity to the Gulf Stream and the sea. When it did we fashioned all sorts of devices to use as sleds, from bent up galvanised metal sheets, to trays and bits of timber. My father, whose hobby was woodwork, built me a real sled from a plan in *Hobbies* magazine. It was a flyer, but as luck would have it, on almost the very first outing, I crashed into the cut-down stub of a large tree, which had a long spike of timber left sticking out where the tree had broken off when cut down. This spike inserted itself under my kneecap at the side and I couldn't get out of it. Eventually my friends had the bright idea of reversing me and the sled out from under the stub, with me now screaming like a banshee, as the pain finally kicked in. My blood was gushing over the snow staining it bright red and making us all think that I was in danger of bleeding to death.

They pulled and dragged the sled with me aboard, leaving a trail of my blood in the snow until they got to our house, whereupon my mother cleaned it up to reveal quite a small hole about half an inch long. As luck would have it, our doctor, the renowned Dr McHale was in the neighbourhood visiting somebody sick with the flu and when he took a look at it he cleaned it again with some surgical spirit and stuck a large sticking plaster on it and told me I would be better before I was twice married. Of course he was right. My knee was stiff for a couple of days and apart from a small scar, which I still carry as a souvenir, I suffered no other ill effects for my adventure.

During these winter months another hobby was sliding on the ice, but since there was rarely enough frost to really freeze our pond to support us, we took to throwing water on the footpath in lower Salthill from the front of Ward's Hotel as far as the entrance gates to St Joseph's Boys Industrial School. This was a fairly new footpath of very smooth concrete, with a fall of about two feet in its fifty or sixty yards length and when we had skated over it for a bit, it would polish up nicely and become highly slippery. We would have great fun here lining up and taking our turns with our hobnailed soles, but for the unfortunate citizens of this street, many of them elderly, it meant that it was totally impassable. The Christian brothers would come out and throw salt on it or sometimes ashes, thereby rendering it useless and we would have to wait until the next frosty night to get it working again.

We all played Cad, with a long stick, a short pointed stick and two stones. This was a complicated game in which a short stick about six inches long with two pointed ends was placed across two stones, and using a long stick as a type of club it would be scooped as far away from the stones as possible. The long stick was then placed on the stones and your opponent had to knock this off using the short stick from the exact point at which it fell. If they succeeded then it was their turn, if not then you were allowed to strike the short stick on one of its pointed end which made it rise, spinning, into the air, and then again with the long stick if you had the skill you could hit it, cricket bat style, as far away as you could and they had to try all over again.

The girls played Hop Scotch as I mentioned before and other games such as hide and seek were day-long affairs 'up the fields' where there were square miles of hiding area and acres of bushes and trees in which to hide. At night if we were allowed out we played a game called 'Jack, Jack show the light'.

Another game was 'One two three red light', in which the caller had his back to the assembled crowd and would spin around on the word red light and try to catch anybody moving toward him. The object of the game was to touch him thereby becoming the caller for the next game. There were other more basic but similar games, such as 'Statues', in which the participants had to freeze in what-ever position they were without moving, on pain of being sent back to the start again if they failed. Another version was 'Giant Steps' and of course there was always tag, which we, for some reason I'll never know, called tig.

Older boys surreptitiously played pitch and toss with pennies, calling heads or harps (tails) since our Irish money had a harp on the reverse. This was seen as a form of gambling and was very much frowned upon. We younger kids were not even allowed to watch by our parents for fear, heaven forbid, that we might become gam-blers, or by the older boys who participated for fear we'd snitch on them. We still got to see the odd game though and personally I thought it was a great waste of good pennies.

One of the big weeks of the year was race week or the Galway races and this gave rise to another curious but engrossing pastime, we called taking numbers.

In those days, still during the war, there was little or no mechanical traffic on the roads and so it was necessary for people to come to Galway a few days early to be sure to get accommodation. This had the effect of doubling or even trebling the population of the city and it was the time of the year when local hotels, guest houses, bed and breakfast places, bars, restaurants, dance halls and shops made the money which was to see them through the following winter.

It had another unexpected effect also, in that it caused a resurrection of the horse and horse-drawn transport, for the week of the races, although in those days it was only Wednesday and Thursday that were the race days with a further day on Friday in Tuam. For this week every single horse-drawn vehicle that could be imagined descended on Galway. There were traps, those bucket shaped open single horse vehicles with seating for about four or five people inside, entered through a door on the back. There were shooting brakes, which were a larger four-wheeled version of the trap which could accommodate about ten or twelve people sitting face to face on two long benches, with the driver and his mate sitting high in front, and were pulled by two strong horses.

There were a few fancy landaulets – light, fast, streamlined vehicles with tops that could be closed pram-like when rain threatened and even a few coaches, but above all the most numerous by far were the side cars, or to give them their full title, outside cars. These were perilously high vehicles, which could accommodate six passengers, three to a side, who sat back to back on the centre seat, with their legs hanging over the side and resting in a box-like device that hung down on both sides. The driver sat in the front of this seat and drove the single horse. This was the sort of cart on which Mickileen brought John Wayne and Maureen O'Hara out courting in the film *The Quiet Man*.

Every one of these vehicles had by law to carry a licence number and also the name and address of its operator written where it was plain to see. Some of these signs were very well painted by professional sign writers, while others were pretty amateur efforts painted by the operator himself or by his children.

For the duration of the race week we would happily sit on top of the old estate wall at the entrance to Devon Park, armed with copybooks and pencils meticulously recording every single number we could get and describing the vehicle that carried it. I don't know why we did this, we just did and later when motorcars came back on the roads we recorded their numbers also. The trick was to have the most numbers and you weren't allowed to record the same number twice. As the races drew closer there were more and more of these vehicles on the road. They ran day and night, hauling people from Galway City to Salthill to see the sea or hauling those who had seen it into Galway for the shops, or to go to the races, or whatever. During the night they continued relentlessly hauling drinkers from Salthill to Galway, who sang at the moon as they rode, or just bawled their heads off with the sheer exhilaration of being free, drunk and at the races.

The numbers collected ran into hundreds and if even one of the lists survived until today, it might provide a really valuable window into the past, but for the same reason as we collected them, once the races had passed, we discarded the lists and went on to do something else.

7. The Flicks

—॥॥—

By far the favourite summer game that we played was Cowboys and Indians, influenced heavily by whatever film we had seen at the Estoria in the Sunday matinee – especially the serial or 'follier upper' in which Charles Starret, or the Durango Kid or Hopalong Cassidy came within seconds of death at the end of every episode.

The Estoria was pretty much the centre of our universe on Sundays, as that was the day that the kids' matinee was played. There would be a matinee on Saturday too but that was not as popular. On Sundays there would be a short two-reeler if we were lucky, featuring Laurel and Hardy, or Charlie Chase, or Ben Turpin (he of the crossed eyes). Next there would be an episode of the serial and these varied from cowboys such as those mentioned above, or tales of daring-do in which the hero Smiling Jack Martin, aviator and secret agent, risked all to rescue some stupid girl who kept getting herself into mortal danger every single week. There were jungle serials in which fierce natives battled with the good guys, who were always white and always wore white shirts, just as the good-guy cowboys always wore white hats. In one of these jungle series I recall the aforementioned Galway-born actor Seán McGlory as a white hunter, roaring at his pygmy henchmen in what purported to be the local pygmy dialect, but was actually Irish. We howled with laughter as he shouted "Brostaigh! Brostaigh!" to them, which means "Hurry! Hurry!" in Gaelic. It gave us an imagined edge over the worldwide audiences who might expect that it was actually some strange jungle dialect.

After the serial there would be a cartoon and then Movietone News, which were always very biased in favour of the allied forces and told us how the good guys were defeating the Nazis and the Japs. Following an interval, to allow us to buy more sweets, came the major feature. Again this was always some sort of a thriller. Romance bored us and if the good guy kissed the girl there would be whistles and shouts and catcalls to get on with the picture and worldly-wise comments from the older boys. This uproar inevitably drew the usher on us with his or her flashlight picking us out in the darkness together with admonitions to be quiet or we'd be thrown out, something that did actually happen from time to time, especially if there was a big crowd waiting for seats outside, whereupon the seat would be sold again and the unfortunate ejectee would get no refund.

The head honcho of the Estoria was a man called Rafter and his buddy was the projectionist. Rafter was an extremely nice man really as I found out when I got older, but to us when we were kids he was the enemy. He was follically challenged as we would say nowadays and to us he was always known as Baldy. He and his side kick liked to go for an odd pint together and when the heat would tempt them on a summer Sunday, they would rush to Helly's Bar, a distance of about two or three hundred yards just after loading on a reel. This gave them about fifteen minutes and they timed it to a tee.

Unfortunately for them from time to time the carbon arc would begin to die and the picture would get darker and darker with nobody to turn the trimmer handle and there would be howls for Baldy to turn on the lights. This would provoke frenzy from the ushers and could end up with several kids being ejected. Often of course they would arrive back just in time and the arc would recover with blinding brilliance. Only once do I remember a reel actually running out.

Sometimes, there would be great confusion in the story line when fellows who had died early on would be alive again, or they would be burying somebody who had died unbeknownst to us. The answer to this riddle came to me when my parents once brought me to a night performance of a film I had seen earlier in the day because they could get nobody to baby-sit and would not risk leaving me alone again. In the night show there were less short films and the main feature made perfect sense. This was because they had shown the entire film in the night show while, to save time for themselves, they had dropped a reel during the matinee, knowing that we would hardly miss it. I never trusted them fully after that and made sure to tell all my pals what the film was really about the next day.

Sometimes one of us, for one reason or the other, couldn't get to go to a picture and what we did on those occasions was to go to one of our mates who had been to the particular film and ask him to "Tell us the picture". This required a very special skill and most of us could do it. The narration would be accompanied by vocal impressions of gunshots and explosions and airplane noises and gestures such as shooting or flying with arms outstretched, the love scenes, if there were any, would be dismissed as "that auld love rubbish" and the exciting highlights would be pointed up with even a little exaggeration. If there were two people trying to tell you the picture sometimes there would be arguments of interpretation, but if they were good you got an even better version.

The very first film I ever saw was the cartoon *Pinocchio* and I was terrified of the fate that was befalling him with the wolf and delighted when Jiminy Cricket saved him. The next film I saw was in Westport with my cousins and the whole family and this was the wonderful *The Wizard of Oz* in which the young Judy Garland starred. My aunt bought the sheet music of the songs from the film and they very quickly became part of our repertoire. I still get flashbacks to this time whenever I hear the song *Somewhere over the Rainbow*.

It was action films and cowboy films that were our staple diet at the Estoria. I recall several upbeat, gung-ho war films, which were made I suppose as propaganda to convince an American population at war that things were going well and they were in no danger of losing. These films, such as *Back to Bataan* and *The Sands of Iwo Jima*, featured actors such as John Wayne who single-handedly, either as tough marines or fighter pilots, were fighting back and winning the war against the yellow peril – something they were actually to achieve before long. In these films the Japanese pilots were never as good as the Yanks and inevitably there would be one of them with his oriental eyes encased in thick goggles and wearing a leather helmet who never failed to say "Die Yankee dog" as he dived into battle only to be shot down or blown to bits. We always cheered at this, which shows, I suppose, what a good propaganda tool these films really were.

Other films to stick in my mind were *Lassie Come Home* in which a brave and faithful dog got lost and followed his young owner across hundreds of miles of strange country, evading villains and disaster only to turn up unscathed in the end. There were also the swashbuckling specials of Errol Flynn such as *Captain Blood*, or our all-time favourite *They Died With Their Boots On*, which told the tale of the arrogant General Custer and the hapless American 7th Cavalry who got their comeuppance from Chief Sitting Bull and the Sioux nation. The tune *Garryowen* which was Custer's marching tune became our anthem whenever playing games which featured the U.S. Cavalry, and they often appeared in our games of Cowboys and Indians, arriving over the hill just in time to save the day.

Another firm favourite were the Johnny Weissmuller *Tarzan* films, which we played in our own jungle up the fields with ropes hanging from strong branches to take the place of vines on which to swing from tree to tree. We didn't think much of Jane though, even though she was played by Irish actress Maureen O'Sullivan, as we felt she slowed up the action and was always getting into trouble and needing rescuing. We felt that Tarzan would really have been much better off without her. We were very taken with Cheetah, the almost human chimpanzee, and enjoyed his antics.

The scary films were always to do with slow-walking Egyptian mummies, zombies or Frankenstein, even Dracula. Always accompanied by weird, scary music to set the scene. Lon Chaney with his mournful face and long jowls, who played in many of these parts, was a household name. Of course the special effects in those days were pretty poor compared with today and blood and guts in a black and white movie isn't half as scary as it is in full colour, but we too were much less sophisticated in those days and many were the nights that Lon Chaney caused me to sleep with the light on.

Apart from the spectacular big films like *The Wizard of Oz,* mentioned earlier, and *Gone with the Wind,* which I saw with my parents, most of the films we saw were in black and white. Cheap two reelers or three reelers, B movies and second features even third features were our staple diet. We loved *Our Gang* and as I bore a passing resemblance to Spanky, for a time I was in danger of carrying this as a nickname. In fact Harold Lewis, the driver of the Galway-Ballina Bus, which used to bring us to Westport, called me this for many years afterwards. Other firm favourites were the *East Side Kids* who metamorphosed later into *The Bowery Boys* and Leo Gorcey and Huntz Hall who played Slip Mahoney and Satch respectively, were the funniest guys imaginable, especially Slip who always used big words he didn't understand. I can still see him telling his gang, "We will now sympathise our watches". I used to do a passable imitation of him with one of my father's old hats turned up in the front while a mate of mine, Noel Dowley, wearing a baseball cap with a turned up peak, was a very convincing Satch, but that was a bit later in life.

The good guys in the cowboy pictures apart from always wearing white hats always had a funny sidekick that played the comic foil to their straight buddies. Thus Gabby Hayes was Roy Rogers's wizened and bearded sidekick while Fuzzy Knight with his horse Ringeye (the white horse had a black ring around his right eye) was foil, I think, to Hopalong Cassidy or maybe Charles Starret, I forget which. One of our gang could do a good imitation of Gabby Hayes and such was his prowess that the name Gabby stuck to him for life amongst those of us who knew him.

In those days the fours, or four penny seats (front stalls) were our kingdom, but as we grew older and started to have notions about girls and stuff, we moved up to the nine penny seats into the back stalls and even the balcony which was still only nine pence. But I get ahead of myself. Sometimes when the lights went off some of the lads would run up in the dark along the back of the seats as far as the back stalls which were much more comfortable than the fours. If they were caught they were returned with indignity to their own seats or else ejected.

Getting and holding on to four pence was a major feat as the weekly allowance of most of us was usually only six pence, or at most a shilling. In the war years there was sugar rationing so there weren't too many sweets or chocolates to be had and fruit was seasonal since only Irish fruit could be bought. We still found ways of spending our pocket money and for me comics were my other addiction. Apart from the aforementioned *Beano* and *Dandy,* I had by now graduated to *Film Fun,* which featured Laurel and Hardy on the front page, and *Radio Fun,* which had Arthur Askey or Tommy Hanley of I.T.M.A fame on the front cover. These comics had pages with stories in text as well as comic cartoons and soon, as I grew older I progressed to the Irish comic *Our Boys* and other 'reading comics' such as *The Hotspur* and *The Wizard.* Occasionally too there would be the odd American comic, with *Superman* and *Captain Marvel,* which would arrive in parcels from America to various families and these were traded and guarded as very special treasures indeed.

Thinking back I feel that our exposure to the culture of America and to a lesser extent England through the medium of the cinema and also through these comics was the start for us of a realisation that there was a big world out there in which things were different from here at home and we longed for a time when we would be able to go and see America for ourselves. Of course, our vision of America was that of Cowboys and Indians and Cops and Robbers, big fancy cars loaded with chrome carrying gangsters with Tommy guns and giant steam trains that had cow catchers on their fronts and rang a bell instead of the shrill steam whistle that our trains had. Many of those lads from my childhood eventually got to see America and England at first hand out of necessity and most of them never came back, but that's another story.

8. The Bish

—∿∿—

In 1943, I grew too old for the Presentation convent school and so I moved up to the Bish, which was the same school my father had attended. The Bish (an abbreviation of Bishop's) was operated by the Patrician Brothers and was located in Nun's Island opposite the present secondary school, which is still called the Bish. For me this was going to be a great change as it was the first time that I was going to be in an all male class and to be taught by men and I wasn't sure if I liked the idea. I needn't have worried for the first two teachers I had were gentle men in every sense of the word. Brother Majella taught first class and he was a kind considerate man who loved children.

One of the first things I remember learning from him were the Latin responses that were required in those days to serve mass and when I had passed them to his satisfaction I became a mass server in Salthill Church, but more about that later. The school building itself was a pretty primitive affair with large, high, cold classrooms and great big rattling windows which let in draughts and let out any heat that the single fire in each classroom might have generated. The floors were wooden and the benches were long timber affairs with cast iron legs screwed to the floor. Each bench held about eight or nine boys and there were five or six rows of them as the classes in those days were very big.

The toilets were outside, a row of about ten red brick cubicles which were cantilevered out over a millstream of the River Corrib. If you looked down through the hole in the seat it was possible to see the river rushing past below and this provided an instant flushing service; though not a very hygienic one for those further downstream. Needless to mention with several hundred boys in the school there were many misses, so finding a clean place to park was a tricky operation. The urinals ran in front of the cubicles and were simply a concrete plastered wall with a red terracotta half pipe at the end of it and a few desultory automatic flushers that didn't do a very thorough job, so an acrid ammonia-like smell was very prevalent. However, it is fair to say that these toilets were as good as anywhere else at this time. Care and concern for the environment hadn't yet become the industry it is today.

I've already mentioned the heating for the classrooms, which was provided by a single fire. Since fuel of any sort was very hard to come by in these war years, necessity became the mother of invention and anthracite balls fuelled the fires. The anthracite was a native product that came, I think, from arigna in the form of crushed chips not much bigger than dust. This had to be made into balls by mixing it with a light coating of cement dust and some water and then pressed firmly between the hands in the manner of making snowballs. These had to be laid aside and allowed to dry before they could be used as a very poor fuel. Every boy in the school had to have a go at this very messy job regardless of his age or circumstances. Needless to mention it required a certain amount of skill and a lot of pressure to make them right, so certain boys were better at making them than others and they got to dodge a lot of class time. One boy in particular called, I think, Pádraic Clancy got to do the job almost full time. The brothers would light the fires, which took a special skill considering the fuel, at about eight o'clock in the morning, so that by the time we got there at nine, there would be a semblance of heat in the room. This vanished pretty quickly though as the frozen, often wet, bodies crowded around before the class started and once the class began the teacher would take up his place of honour right in front of the fire ensuring that very little of the heat got past him. I remember one particular lay teacher whose trousers legs were scorched from bum to the cuffs from this practice.

Next to the routine educational subjects, the most important thing in the Bish was the choir. This was the realm of Brother Cuthbert, a musician to his fingertips with an almost fanatical love and devotion to music and to choral music in particular. To this end, every single boy who joined the school was screened and tested to see if he had a voice and if he did he was immediately sent to Brother Cuthbert for induction into the choir. Being a fairly passable soprano in those days I was in almost on my first day but I didn't have it all my own way as, unlike the Presentation School, the Bish was up to its eyes in sopranos. I made it into the front row with the first sopranos, alongside Jimmy Gleeson, Pat Broderick and Frank Kelly who had been there before me. All three of them were great sopranos and together we made up a formidable front row.

When the choir training began, Brother Cuthbert would have his sidekick, the sometimes sadistic Brother Oliver, wander around with his ear cocked listening to see if any crows had managed to infiltrate the choir. If a bum note was heard the perpetrator was hauled out unceremoniously by his ear, literally, then given a boot in the backside and told to scram and not to be wasting Brother Cuthbert's time. This was a pretty harsh rejection and boys would often be perspiring as they sang for fear of the grab. As Brother Oliver passed among them you could see them mentally flinching away. If this seems like harsh treatment today, it was the norm in those days and slaps and clouts were an everyday part of life. In the back garden of the house next door to the Bish, the O'Regan family had an ash tree and every now and then a boy would be sent out to break a small branch off to bring back into the class so that the teacher in question could fashion it into a weapon of punishment.

Back to the choir; every year in Galway there were several choral competitions, there was the liturgical one at which only church music could be sung which was performed in the Pro Cathedral and the Feis Ceoil an Iarthair at An Taibhdhearc at which choirs had to sing one song in Irish and were also allowed to sing one in English. This was the major event in Br Cuthbert's calendar and we spent the year working towards it. Two of the big numbers I remember were *The Blue Danube* and the chorus of the Hebrew slaves from Verdi's *Nabuccho,* called *Va pensero,* which we sang in Italian. To this day I can remember every nuance and every word of both of them and remember the joy of singing them when they were ready, but also the fear and trembling for fear of making a mistake while rehearsing them. It was my introduction to proper classical singing and, with the benefit of hindsight, I can say that it was here I fell in love with choral and operatic music. Of course individual sopranos were prepared by Brother Cuthbert for the Feis as well and, one by one, all of the three aforementioned boys and myself were entered and won the first prize. Pat Broderick won more often than the rest of us as he had an extremely powerful Maria Callas type voice for one so young.

The procedure in the Bish once we got to first class was for a teacher to join us at that stage and stay with us for the next four years until we were at the primary exam stage. This was a good idea, for in the interim the teacher would get to know us, and vice versa, and a mutual respect or fear would develop. We were extreme-ly lucky in our class to get Cyril Mahoney. He was enlightened bookish man who had a passion for teaching, a wonderful sense of humour and he actually liked us. He was, in later life, to become one of my best friends. In addition to teaching he was a part-time actor at An Taibhdhearc and was dedicated to the Irish language. He was also an officer in the L.D.F., which was the Irish equivalent of the Territorial Army in England or the national reserve in the USA. On parade days he would turn up looking very smart in his officer's uniform and I remember an occasion when he frightened the life out of us by juggling a couple of hand grenades, which he knew to be dummies but which we did not.

His approach to teaching was encouragement and reward. This

was in marked contrast to two other masters behind us in the school at the time who believed that all education could be driven in by the use of a stick or a fist. We would gasp with relief when we could hear these other masters administer their particular brand of rough justice or torture through the flimsy pine and glass partitions that separated the classes. We all knew how lucky we were to have drawn Cyril as our master. Of course he also had to punish us from time to time, as that was the way of things in those days, but he did it in such an innovative way and with such good humour it didn't seem to hurt as much.

His tactic was to line all those due for punishment for whatever reason out along the wall of the classroom and at the end of the class he would make a big drama about taking off his jacket, rolling up his shirt sleeves, spitting on his hand for strength and running with the cane along the shins of the standing boys like a child might run a stick along a set of railings. When he reached the end, he would repeat his pantomime and return again along the shins form the other direction. If a boy tried to avoid it by lifting his leg he would give them one on the knee and continue. This hurt of course for a little time, but it was nothing to the brutal lashing of ash plant on bare hands that we could hear regularly from the next class. One of the other teachers had been a boxer at one time and was known by the class as 'The Boxer'. On one occasion he actually knocked a young boy out with a punch to the face. The boy's father was a pretty influential local businessman and he sought redress and I seem to remember got an apology. Fortunately for the school and the particular teacher, Ireland was not a litigious place back in those days.

If a boy was injured or not too seriously hurt the procedure was to send them down with another boy as an escort to Whelan's Chemists in Dominick Street. Mister Whelan, who was a pharmacist acted as an impromptu doctor, counsellor, nurse and general hospital for all the ailments that befell us. My turn to visit him came when the boy sitting next to me, Dessie Ward, helped me out one day by topping my pencil, which had broken for the umpteenth time. It was forbidden for boys to have sharp implements for obvious reasons, but Dessie being a free spirit, was the proud possessor of a so-called safety razor blade. So that the teacher wouldn't see us, I held the pencil under the desk while he topped it, unfortunately he was feigning attention to the teacher while so doing and managed to give me an inch-long slice on the index finger of my left hand. Suddenly there was blood everywhere and people were jumping up to get out of the way. Cyril was on us like a flash and read the situation. By now the bloody razor was on the floor so it was not possible to say which of us was using it. He wrapped his clean handkerchief around my finger and Dessie and I were sent post haste to Whelan's for first aid, me for first aid and Dessie as my escort. I got a terrific big plaster that went all around my finger and when we returned we were kept in to see which of us owned the blade. Firstly we both said neither of us owned it, and then we said that both of us owned it. Since there was no resolution to the riddle we were both punished and that was that. I still carry the mark on my finger to remind me of this incident.

Penmanship was very important to all educators in those days and we used headline copy books which we had to copy as well as we could, so many lines per night. The preferred pen was an 'N' pen which was I think a particular make, or maybe it was a special dimension. This N pen was oxidised a sort of greenish brown colour and slipped onto a wooden handle, about the same length as a pencil. It was dipped into an inkwell, which was a little white ceramic dish let into a hole in the desk in front of every pupil. Like the fuel for the fire, this ink had to be made by us boys, by first of all putting a sort of dark goo, which I think was a mixture of gum Arabic and indigo, into a large bottle and filling the required amount of water in, before capping it with a hand and shaking vigorously. Some boys made weak ink, which dried almost invisibly, others made ink that was too strong and had a copperish tinge. One boy, who shall remain nameless, put a drop of Dettol through it to see what would happen and the result was that the ink spread out as if it were on blotting paper. Needless to mention he paid for his prank and was further forced to empty out every inkwell in the school, wash them thoroughly under the tap in the yard and, having replaced them in all the two hundred or so desks, refill them with proper ink. I think he went on to do Chemistry in later life.

The ceilings of the classrooms were high, about twelve feet or so and were sheeted in pitch pine and varnished. A nasty little game that was prevalent in my time, and apparently for a long time before that, was to steal a boy's pen and throw it dart like at the ceiling. If your aim was good it stuck there and your unfortunate victim was penless, unless he happened to have a spare. If you were caught doing this the punishment was swift and deadly and you might have to forfeit your own pen to replace that of your victim. Of course, if the teacher wasn't about during a break, it was possible to launch a book at the ceiling, thereby dislodging a few pens in the hope that one of them might survive unbroken or not too badly damaged so that it might be bent back into shape. These seldom worked as well as new ones but might get you out of trouble with the master for not doing your writing or whatever tasks you might have to write down.

In the rough concrete yard we played tig, football and handball against the school gable and whatever other diversion was common at the time. One boy, nicknamed Flats, caused no small consternation when, having attended the show of the well known hypnotist Paul Goldin, who was appearing in the Town Hall at the time, discovered that he too had the ability to hypnotise people. All of a sudden boys would be going around barking like dogs, clucking like chickens, or facing up to the teachers and refusing to sit down or to do whatever they were told. It took the Brothers a couple of days to find out what was going on and then to trace the culprit and when they did their vengeance was awesome. He was forbidden on pain of expulsion from ever doing it again and as far as I know, he never did. It was a pity really because he was pretty good at it.

Now that I was that bit older, I was allowed to go home for my lunch, instead of bringing it in a bag with me as I had done in the Pres. This meant catching the bus at O'Brien's Bridge at about three minutes past one, so there would be an scramble from the classroom once the bell rang at about a minute or two to one everyday. Some days, the wind would be from the south and the fumes and smell from the sulphuric acid plant of the nearby McDonogh chemical factory would have us coughing and spluttering and our eyes watering. There was scant attention to health and safety in those days. If the bus could be seen to have arrived at the O'Brien's Bridge stop, we had to leg it as far as the next stop at Whelan's chemist shop in Dominick Street and head it off there, as it had to weave its way through the concrete and iron tank traps that were positioned on O'Brien's Bridge to prevent the Germans from invading the city. This assumed of course that the Germans were going to attack us from the west, as there were no such tank traps on the eastern or northern side of the town. Later it transpired that these tank traps might equally have been used to prevent attack by allied forces, since at the time there was a fear that Ireland's neutrality was such a bone of contention to Churchill and his American allies that there might be an attempt by them to recover the seaports for use against the German U Boats.

The red and white buses, which were operated by the Great Southern Railway Company cost us schoolboys a halfpenny from town to Devon Park and took about ten minutes. By going home at lunchtime it meant that my father, mother and myself could have our dinner together, which my mother would have waiting on the table as we walked in the door. This arrangement also meant that she was now finished cooking and freed up for her music pupils who began to arrive after lunchtime. My father cycled from wherever he was working in the city to arrive at the same time as me. Sometimes if I finished my lunch early I would manage to walk or even run back to school in time and save the halfpenny for other uses. Sometimes also, Mr Geraghty, the father of three boys attending the Bish, who had a government job and was entitled to petrol, would pile as many of us as he could into his Model 'A' Ford motor car and give us a lift both ways. This would save us a whole penny on those occasions. There could be three layers of us in the back but nobody seemed to mind; free transport was free transport.

In the beginning when first we moved to Devon Park, the bus would stop anywhere you put up your hand, but as the number of passengers increased this caused too many delays and so certain spots were designated as bus stops. These were indicated with the word bus painted on the road in white paint. This was fine when the paint was fresh but gradually the paint would wear away and only local knowledge could inform you of where they were. This was okay for us, since we knew where they were, but hell for the occasional tourist, so eventually after a couple of years of this they wrote the word bus on a black pointed metal sign, nowadays known as finger signs and nailed them to convenient E.S.B. poles. This lasted until the company was taken over by C.I.E. and then they were forced by the E.S.B. to remove the signs and put up proper bus stop signs on small metal poles of their own, which ranged from black and white striped to silver.

In those days personal hygiene was not what it was today. To be fair, it wasn't easy for many boys, as many of the houses then didn't even have inside plumbing. So in this environment many nasty things could happen. One of the most frequent epidemics, if it could be called that, was the outbreak of head lice or nits as they were known. The County Medical Officer would then decree that all boys in the offending school would have to get their hair cut right to the bone, in the manner of a 'number one' today. The alternative was a letter from your mother to say that she personally undertook to wash and fine comb your hair every day until the outbreak was finished. My mother, for some reason was rather proud of my hair and refused to give me a cropping and so for weeks on end I would have to suffer the excruciating torture of the fine-tooth comb. This tiny comb had teeth which were sharp, set very close together and would be dragged along the actual scalp, slanted in such away that any 'boodies' as they were called would be trapped in between them. My mother was very painstaking and thorough in her diligence to get at any nits and so every evening after washing and drying my hair this ritual dragged on for nearly a half and hour. Personally I would have preferred the crew cut, since I was one of the few who didn't have one at school and we were teased as 'mammy's boys'. It's always dangerous to be different.

During these years, apart from the outbreak of nits, there were many other maladies which appeared to come in waves and which many or all of us got as a matter of routine. We got measles, mumps and chicken pox, but if my memory serves me we had been inoculated by the Galway County Medical Officer or one of his doctors beforehand to prevent any serious after effects. Those less fortunate of us got scarlet fever and I think some typhoid and there was even a case of diphtheria. We had all been vaccinated against polio, so thankfully in our time there were no instances of this dreaded disease. None of us knew what these diseases did, so naturally the wise guys had tales of horror and said that your throat turned black and blue and you choked to death if you got diphtheria. We were in terror of this happening, but fortunately none of us got to experience it.

The doctor visited school on a regular basis to give us whatever inoculation or vaccination was the flavour of the month. We lived in fear and trembling of these days, knowing that for sure somebody was going to come and stick a needle in us before the end of the day and that it would hurt. They always hurt in those days. I remember one such treatment though, which might have been the polio vaccine, which caught us all by surprise as it was poured on to a sugar lump and sucked. We all loved that one. The dreaded school dentist also came along with depressing regularity and really scared us and hurt us too. These were not gentle souls who gave you sympathy and little fillings if you had a cavity. They stuck a mountainous needle in your gums and with something that resembled pliers they hauled out the offending molar, washing your mouth afterwards with salt and water. The only good thing about the dentists visit was that if you had been treated you got to go home and have the rest of the day off.

The one school visitor that really struck terror into us all though was the school guard (policeman). Guard Murphy was the official truancy officer for Galway City and would come on a regular basis and sit at the head of the classroom going through the roll books and eyeing us in a threatening manner out from under his very large bushy eyebrows. He was a very tall, square-faced man, something in the region of six foot two or three, with quite a high-pitched voice and he spoke in an accent that indicated his southern origins. I can honestly say with hand on heart that I never in my life played truant, or mitched, or 'went on the beryl' as we used to say. Nevertheless, if you had been out sick for a couple of days there would be a couple of blank spaces in the roll book and he would make a great production of asking you where you had been and if you really were sick and if your mother had written a note for the teacher and so on. Of course, the primary purpose was to deter us from the notion of mitching rather than punishing us, since I must say there was very little of it done in our class anyway, probably because we enjoyed our teacher Cyril Mahoney.

The punishment for consistent truancy was being sent to Letterfrack Industrial School, which even in those days instilled fear and terror into all who had heard tales of the terrible fate that awaited boys out there in that remote part of Conamara. There were apocryphal tales of boys who had mitched from school for a couple of days who had been caught and sentenced to a year out there in the wilds of Conamara and had never come back home again, that brothers had beaten them and starved them. Nobody in his right mind would ever dream of getting sent to Letterfrack, yet, sad to say, many boys did, although not any that I can remember from our school. Sad to say, in recent years it has transpired that many of the tales of Letterfrack Industrial School were, unfortunately, true and it has been at the centre of many of the child abuse cases that are now surfacing in courts around the land.

There was a great rivalry between schools in sports, theatrical and musical events. The Patrician brothers ran a sister school to ours in Lombard street called the Monastery (or amongst ourselves, the Mon) for inner city boys and there was a school in Claddagh for children from that area, while there was a lay school in Woodquay called St. Brendan's for boys from Bohermore and Hidden Valley as parts of it were known. The Jesuits ran a school in Sea Road that catered for boys whose parents were more well to do. These we considered to be stuck up snobs. Whenever an opportunity arose at which we could beat them, whether in hurling or football or choral competitions or any other competition we were delighted, though at national school level I must admit they were better at hurling than most other schools, while we had the edge on them in most other competitions, especially the choral ones.

Within the Bish and the other schools there was also rivalry between the different districts in the town and it might be that at lunch time you would be told that the Claddaghs and the Shannies were going to attack Devon Park the following Saturday after school. This was considered as a challenge to war and so the following Saturday afternoon the Devon Parkers together with a few allies from Lenaboy Park and other Salthill areas would lay in a supply of stones and sticks and any other weapon that would prove useful up the fields. We had a few older boys who understood strategy and on one occasion I recall that John Sheridan was at home on leave from the R.A.F. and, although in his twenties, he agreed to help us out with our war. We knew that the Claddaghs would attack us from over the hill in the football pitch because they could get there without having to walk past our houses, so John had us line the sides of the pitch in the bushes and he set up about ten lads to draw the fire and encourage them to attack down the centre of the pitch where they would have no cover.

We used catapults, or 'cathys' as we called them, in the main, although in later years there were a few snipers with bb shot and pellet guns in our group. These consisted of a Y shaped fork of wood to which were attached two strips of rubber, usually the red rubber from motor car inner tubes and a leather pouch joining them at the back which held the stone. Some of the good marksmen could hit targets with them at about a hundred yards, but at fifty yards they were deadly accurate. The Claddaghs, although they used some catapults, favoured the sling, a weapon as old as mankind and one that, in the hands of an expert, was deadly. The sling consisted of two lengths of cord, sometimes leather thongs, about two feet or more long, joined at the centre by a leather pouch similar to the catapult, but larger. A stone was put into this pouch and the whole thing, using the momentum of the stone, was spun around your head until sufficient force had been generated, at which time one of the strings would be released and the stone would fly in the required direction with amazing force. This was the artillery of the gang war. There were guys in Claddagh who could part your hair with a stone as big as your fist from about one hundred yards away.

This was the reason for the war strategy then, to get them in close where the slings would be less useful and less accurate. It worked like a dream and they attacked down the centre, right past us and when they had arrived at the centre of the pitch, the guys they were chasing turned and attacked back, only by then we had come up from our hiding places in the bushes on their flanks and to their rear and with devastating 'cathy' fire, forced them to flee down the only avenue we had left open for them, as it is always good to allow the enemy to escape in these circumstances or else you may have to fight hand to hand with them and none of us wanted that as they were much tougher than us.

Of course not all of our battles were this successful, as we didn't always have a strategist on our side and very often we lost, falling back into our back yards where we knew they wouldn't follow or fire for fear of breaking windows, for the law was still the law in those days and nobody wanted that. When we did this we were called 'yella bellies' but we preferred to think of it as a strategic withdrawal. The following day we would all be back at school as if nothing had happened and the post mortems of the fight would be exaggerated on both sides and the taunting and joking would fizzle out in the face of the next piece of excitement whatever that was.

9. Faith of our Fathers

—◊—

One of the major outings of the year was the Eucharistic procession. This took place on the nearest Sunday to the feast of Corpus Christi, which took place on the Thursday following Pentecost or Whit Sunday. This was by far the biggest assembly of people that could be mustered in the city. It commenced in the playing fields of St. Mary's College with an open air mass. This mass was celebrated by the bishop of Galway, Dr. Michael Browne, a stern aloof man who ruled his church with a mixture of iron fist and divine right. Every school in the parish had to assemble with its own banner, large painted and embroidered affairs, similar in size and style though not in message to those now seen in Orange Order parades, held aloft by two and sometimes more carriers, with steadying ropes to prevent them being blown away by the wind. There would be a group of pioneer total abstainers and every church in the parish was also expected to produce a choir, Legion of Mary guild and whatever other group they could. Galway Corporation Councillors in their scarlet and purple robes of office would hold a place of honour.

Following the mass, which would be amplified by Fallon's loudspeakers, the Blessed Sacrament would be carried aloft by the bishop with four priests to assist him, under a canopy of golden cloth supported on four brass poles by the favoured local dignitaries, and surrounded by a guard of honour of army officers, sabres drawn and held at the salute. The procession would file slowly out of St Mary's to the strains of *Faith of our Fathers* played by one of the city's three bands; St Patrick's brass band, the Industrial School brass and reed band or the Dockers fife and drum band, whichever had that honour for that particular year. The Army pipe band would also be there playing away, although they had the difficulty that many of the notes of the hymns did not exist on the pipes and so they would play the nearest note to it, which gave a certain discord to the sound of the hymn and sometimes put the singers off.

When leaving the grounds of St. Mary's the procession would turn left along St. Mary's Road and right down Helen Street and Henry Street, which because of their narrowness would reverberate to the pounding of the drums. Every single household, shop, place of business no matter what, would have an altar with a statue of Christ or Our Lady surrounded by fresh flowers in front of their doors and the streets would be lined with those townspeople not actually in the procession and many country people who would come to town for the day just to pray and to see the spectacle. The route continued up Dominick Street, across O'Brien's Bridge and on up through the main streets of the city until it reached Eyre Square, where it all assembled again in front of another open air altar and the rosary was said and sung. The day was finished off with Benediction and we were all free to find our way home.

Of course the whole thing was a great adventure for us and we all felt very religious and important as we marched along singing hymns and praying until we were nearly hoarse. It was figured by many of us that the bishop had some power over the weather as for some reason the procession always took place on the hottest day of the year. Inevitably the tar would be melting on the roads and our shoes would become covered in this, transferring it to our knees and cloths when we knelt down. I'm sure that these stains irritated many a mother as they required the use of butter to remove them and butter in those days was a scarce commodity only available with coupons. I don't think I ever remember a procession Sunday when it rained.

Throughout the procession there were outriders from the Red Cross and the Knights of Malta, whom we envied in their impressive uniforms complete with water bottles hanging from their belts, and even stretchers to assist those who succumbed to the heat and the pressure of the event. Sore feet and blisters on heels though were more likely to be the main ailments of the day. Funny thing is that in spite of the heat and the amount of walking we had to do none of us would ever have dreamt of bringing a bottle of water to drink along the way. Our group leaders would have been horrified (today one notices that people can hardly walk up town without carrying a bottle of designer water). When the whole thing was over, if you were lucky, one of the bands would be going your way on the way home and they would play more secular marches and you could all march along behind them like soldiers. We marched behind the band of the boys of St. Joseph's Industrial school, under the baton of their leader Mr Fogarty-Kelly and they brought us nearly home. All in all it was a grand day.

Around this time, it was decided I think that the time was ripe for me to put the teachings of Brother Majella to some good and so I was enrolled as a mass server in the nearest church to us, which was Salthill Church. Salthill was a comparatively new church, a satellite church of St. Joseph's parish, and had just recently been completed under the guidance of the energetic Canon Davis, who was parish priest at the time. There were a number of altars and, as many priests came to Salthill for their holidays, the first mass often began at half seven in the morning and continued for the rest of the morning at half hour intervals until eleven. It was common in those days, especially in summer during the school holidays, for boys to serve sometimes three or four masses. Most of us liked doing it and it was considered a good thing to do. We wore a black soutane, with a starched white surplice over it, and black runners on our feet that were especially reserved for serving mass. We prepared the altars, filling the cruets with wine and water before mass

began and lighting the candles. We felt ourselves to be an important part of the mass and we responded to the priest in Latin as he
read the various parts of the mass. We also rang the bell, brought
the water and wine cruets to the altar and helped when commun-
ion was being served by holding a gold plated palette under the
chins of the communicants.

In summer it was quite common to have a priest visiting from
England or America and we loved to serve these because they always
gave us a tip when they were leaving. Of course this was frowned
upon by the local clergy and we weren't supposed to accept these
gratuities, nevertheless, after we had made the rather feeble prot-
estations to the visitors they would insist and we could walk away
with as much as a half a crown for our week's serving. This was
a fabulous amount of money for me, well over twice my weekly
allowance, and so if I could get to serve a few 'Yankee priests' as we
called them I could be made up for the summer. It was important,
however, that you were actually there to receive the money into
your own hand, for if you missed your chance they would leave
it to the sacristan, asking him to pass it on to us, but he very seldom did. He regarded this as an added perk for himself and since
he was an adult we had no choice but to accept this. This is why
we watched the visiting priest like hawks when they were due to
leave and even if we weren't actually serving that morning would be
around to check up on the rosters or other such pretence in a bid
to outwit the Sacristan. He knew that we knew, and we knew that
he knew that we knew, though the cat and mouse game was played
out with neither letting the other know that they understood what
was going on.

On certain Sundays there would be a high Mass and this was a
ceremony filled with terror for us neophytes. It was completely different to the ordinary masses and there would be anything up to
three or four priest and as many as eight or ten servers, each with
a task. In these masses the responses were sung instead of spoken
and the choir had an involvement in the responses, as had we.
There would be incense and blessings and if it fell to you to light
and keep lighting the thurabel, which was the incense burner, you

had to first succeed in making the charcoal light and stay glowing, ensuring that there would be enough to last all through the Mass. Then the thurabel had to be swung at just the right speed to keep the glowing charcoal alight. When the time came to put the incense in you had to open the lid of it, and hold it there until the required amount was sprinkled on the charcoal and then hand it over to the priest just right for the blessing. It was a tense moment for a small boy and one that required a certain amount of rehearsing before the Mass. In the evenings there would be the rosary and benediction and, every now and then, an Adoration of the Blessed Sacrament. This entailed just kneeling there silently for anything up to an hour until the next server relieved you. If he didn't turn up then you had to do his shift too. This was very hard on the knees and required great patience, particularly if it was high summer and you knew that all of your mates were on their way to the beach while you prayed. I suppose it was good for the soul.

Every now and again there would be a wedding and these were our favourites of all the masses, because they were joyous occasions and people were happy and elated during the ceremonies and especially as an envelope would be labelled for the servers and handed over to us after the ceremony. The sacristan got his own envelope so he could not touch ours and on these occasions there would always be a few bob jingling in your pocket on the way home. Perhaps I make this sound as if this was our sole motivation for serving mass but it wasn't, we did it because it was what good young Catholic boys did and we liked to do it. The occasions on which we got any money were few and far between, but it was the responsibility and the ceremony that made it so fulfilling, and the sense that we were somehow or other helping God, even in a small way, or at the very least keeping on his good side.

Funeral masses were sombre occasions so we were expected to be more solemn and silent in our movements on these occasions, especially if the person who had died was known to us or to our parents. The largest and most spectacular funeral mass I ever attended was that for a famous Galway cleric, the Very Reverend Canon Davis, a well loved and respected parish priest, whose mass and funeral were attended by all of the schools in the parish, literally hundreds of children. He was laid to rest beneath the front lawn of the Salthill church, a fitting resting place since he had been the one responsible for its building from start to finish.

Not all our involvement with the religious was positive however; where the mercy nuns were concerned, we were the enemy. At the top end of Devon Park, these nuns had a large orchard. This walled garden was originally the orchard of the O'Hara-Burke estate and covered something in the region of two or more acres. In the centre, on the flat ground there were vegetable ridges, which supplied a ready diet of potatoes and vegetables to the nuns and the girls of the orphanage. A series of gravel pathways crisscrossed the area and all along the pathways were apple trees and pear trees and fruit bushes, which included gooseberries and raspberries as well as blackcurrants and redcurrants. These were our favourite targets, but since they were well away from the large wooden gate, one had to pass by the gardener's gate lodge and risk being spotted.

The gardener was an elderly man called Sheedy, an old-time hardworking countryman, who knew a lot about his job. His main problem was that, being elderly he didn't have the speed to catch us even if we were seen. The walls (being about nine or ten feet) were too high for us to scale and they were topped with shards of broken glass. Since the walls were made of dry masonry, there was one place at the back of the garden where a few stones had fallen away leaving a hole just about large enough to crawl through. The problem with this was that it was in full view of the open garden and trying to enter that way would leave you liable to be caught. Sheedy would block up this hole from time to time but, not having any concrete, it was easy enough to open it again. Our usual tactic was to try to create a distraction in the hope that one of our number could then sneak in the back way and score some apples. This worked well enough and sometimes if we saw Sheedy going up to the convent with vegetables we could slip in and grab whatever presented itself.

On one occasion like this, which turned out to be our last major attack, we were all just in the gate when this shout made us all look up and, running towards us like a greyhound, was a young man aged about thirty or so who had just been hired by the nuns to help Sheedy as assistant gardener. We ran for it across the fields, but fast as we were, he was faster and was gaining on us, until we decided to spilt up and scatter to various hiding places, known to us but not to him. He had great speed and stamina though and continued chasing after two brothers who were running together side by side, each loathe to abandon the other. He grabbed them both by the scruff of their respective necks about half a mile after he began the chase and started back towards the orchard. One of them was young, about eight, and was bawling for his mother, "Maaam! Maaam!" while the other, a couple of years older, was trying to wriggle and kick his way free, shouting all the time for us to come and rescue him. We lay low, not wanting to end up with the same fate. Eventually the new gardener, whose name was Dermot, got them back up to the gate of the orchard and kept them there until Sheedy returned. Sheedy was delighted and pretended that he was going to prosecute them, whatever that meant, and only let the two miscreants go after delivering a very stern warning that the next time we tried anything like this, we would be brought up to the nuns and would end up in the industrial school.

As we got older we found that we could go up to the orchard and actually buy a lot of apples for a few pence, but somehow it wasn't the same as huffing them. Only brave opportunistic solo raids were the order of the day after that, and then only when everybody knew that both Sheedy and Dermot were out of the way. Eventually Dermot got the main gardener job when Sheedy retired, and he got married and lived in the gate lodge for years afterwards. We became good friends later on, but he certainly made the act of huffing apples a lot more dangerous and prevented mass incursion to the nun's orchard from the time he was employed.

10. The Jes

—ᴍᴍ—

As well as teaching the piano, my mother was a particularly fine organist and had begun her career in the Protestant or Church of Ireland Church in Westport. A vacancy occurred for an organist in the Jesuit Church in Sea Road and they heard on the grapevine (and the Jesuits had a better grapevine than most) that my mother could play. She went for an interview, or an audition, and immediately got the job. This delighted her and although the money for such a job was not enough to sustain anybody, it was a stipend and it was her own. Besides, she really did love playing church music. One of the perks of this job was that as her son I was eligible to receive free education in their school. Now this didn't mean any great saving in our family income since the Bish was free anyway, but the Jes though reasonable, was not free and was considered by some to be a more up-market school than the Bish, although I have never subscribed to this theory nor did I ever find anything during my years there that might suggest it to be true.

This occurred just as I reached primary cert, or sixth class and so I was made to go back into the Jes equivalent of sixth class called Bun Rang a Trí A. I was not too pleased at the idea of going back into sixth again, but I was very young and they were not sure how good my Irish was, since everything in the Jes was taught through the medium of Irish. The fact was that my Irish was very good and I had no problems making the transition, at least not from an academic point of view. To the Jes boys though I was a blow-in and from the Bish at that, which meant I was to be regarded with suspicion, while to my old buddies in the Bish I was a traitor, so I spent a few uncomfortable weeks getting used to my new found friends and they to me, as well as reassuring some of my old friends. They were not all strangers to me however since some of the boys from our own neighbourhood were already in the Jes, so through them my bona fides were established.

Now to say that the difference between the Jes and the Bish was as chalk is to cheese would be an understatement. Everything about the school and the approach to teaching was different. In the first instance the Jes was what was known at that time as a Grade A school which meant that everything was taught through the medium of the Irish language only. Fair enough, since I had pretty good Irish anyway, but the school rule was that once you stood on school property, inside the street gate, it was compulsory to speak Irish at all times, to the teachers, the priests and amongst ourselves. I had no problem with this as I was reasonably fluent in Irish but many of my schoolmates had little or no Irish and suffered regularly as a result. Usually if I was punished for English speaking it was to somebody whose Irish wasn't up to scratch. Failure to speak Irish resulted in instant punishment which consisted of anything up to six slaps with a specially constructed, weighted strap. The punishment for this and all other offences was delivered primarily by the Prefect of Studies, Father Eamonn S. Mac Aindrís S.J. or Andy, as he was known by us.

Andy occupied an office inside the main boys' entrance to the school and if and when you were due for punishment, you had to present yourself at his door, charge sheet or chit in hand, which would contain your name, class, offence and punishment recommended. All teachers and priests in the school had to carry a book of these chits, or cheques as some called them, and once they were written and given to you they had to be discharged by Andy.

You knocked timidly at his door, in the off chance that he might not be in there, but he nearly always was. He had a sort of brink-manship game that he rather sadistically played. At the first knock, there would be silence and you would wait with bated breath. You would knock timidly again; still silence and just when you were about to leave with a rising heart he would call "tar isteach!" (come in) and there you were standing on the carpet so to speak in front of his desk. Now the game got into its second phase; he would continue to read his breviary, not looking up at you but leaving you sweating in silence, as he pretended that he had a particularly inter-esting passage to read as the tension mounted. Finally he would carefully mark the page in the breviary and look up at you for the first time over the top of his reading glasses; a look that was meant to cause fear. Then he would reach out his hand for the cheque or chit and read it carefully with a look of painful resignation. If he was in a good mood he would ask you what you had to say for yourself, otherwise he would reach into the cupboard on his right hand side and pull out one of his straps. There were about three straps, one longer than the other and of different weights; each designed to inflict different amounts of pain. The longest one was the worst and a couple of slaps from that would leave your hand numb for ten or fifteen minutes. He selected these as a golfer might select a club, depending on the lie of the ball and then he would come around the desk, flicking the two tails of his soutane over his shoulder so that they might not interfere with his swing, then grabbing your hand he would bring down the strap with all of his might again and again until the recommended punishment had been delivered. When he had finished, he would replace the strap, regain his seat and sign the chit, resuming his religious readings as if he had not been distracted by as much as a fly.

After a few years of this I discovered that I could do a passable copy of his signature and since there was little communication between him and the teachers concerning these matters the decep-tion was not discovered for a long time. When it was, nobody would reveal the identity of the forger, so Andy bought a rubber stamp. We were tempted to buy a rubber stamp too, but by then I only had a year or so to go and it was hardly worthwhile.

The school day began with mass in the boys' chapel and attendance was compulsory, sometimes some of the wide boys would attempt to arrive just as the mass was over and mingle with the crowd coming out, but the Jesuits were not stupid and regularly one or two of the young priests would lurk in the shadows and around corners near the chapel just to catch those likely lads, usually the result was a cheque for the head and four or six slogs to start the day. The only ones exempt were those who had been mass servers earlier in the morning and who had been allowed to cycle home for their breakfasts, but even they were expected to be in time for first class, no matter how far they lived from the school.

Climbing the stairs to the classrooms we passed the various teachers' boxes on the first floor, into which we were required to drop the relevant exercises that we had 'committed' the night before. Sometimes if people had done badly the night before they would drop the exercise copy into the wrong box, thereby getting a breathing space and hoping that the teachers would not exchange the errant copy books. Of course they were wise to this as well and usually they did exchange the copies, but now and again, just once in a blue moon the plan would work and the offending boy would be off the hook, for that evening.

In the Jesuits, sport was as important as education or at least an important part of your education and so no boy was exempt. At the back of the school there was a football/hurling pitch with a running track around it. After school every day there would be football or hurling practice. Under the terms of the so-called 'Grade A' system only Gaelic games would be condoned and even though before this time the Jes had a formidable reputation as a rugby school, (as it has now again) this sport was now forbidden as was anything else which under the G.A.A. banner was known as a foreign game. For most of us this presented no problem in that very few of us had ever played anything else but G.A.A. games.

So, after our drill session in the afternoon we were usually expected to tog out and take part in hurling or football practice depending on the season. I wasn't much good at either but that was no excuse and we all had to go through the motions and turn out for the odd football match or hurling match against the other schools in the city.

St. Mary's Diocesan College and St. Enda's, together with the Bish made up the total schools opposition in the city and many of the lads who attended these colleges were strong country lads who had been reared with a hurley in their hands and so almost inevitably we were hammered. Now and again though we would actually win a match, but to be truthful it was usually due to poor opposition, rather than skill on our part, or certainly on my part.

Once I think I scored a goal in a football match and did such damage to my big toenail in the process that I was unable to walk properly for the next few days. The damage was caused by the goalkeeper who came out to challenge me and drew a kick on the ball at the same time as I did, causing both of our toes to come together with maximum impact. Fortunately for me I had just struck the ball a fraction of a second before and it went into the net before the coming together of the big toes. I recall that the toecap of my football boot was split in two and I was taken off the pitch roaring like the proverbial stuck pig. After that I was less enthusiastic for football.

My hurling experiences weren't much better but I was a big lad and able to defend myself on the pitch and in those days that was half the battle. My sporting career in the Jesuits sort of limped along until a few years later when they introduced rowing and suddenly I was in my element.

But, I get ahead of myself; starting shortly after I joined the school, it was discovered that I was a soprano and while sopranos were as plentiful as the teeth on a comb in the Bish, in the Jes there were none. None of any serious merit that is and it was something that the choirmaster and the head of the schools drama department were lacking. As soon as I arrived I was immediately signed up for the school choir, where I was given all of the solo items to sing, a fact that didn't endear me to the older and longer serving members.

The Jesuits were very interested in theatre and believed that it was a firm part of the education of their boys, so every year there would be a school opera. The first year I arrived I was auditioned for the lead soprano part which was a female role, of course, and while my voice was enough to get the part for me without much bother, I was deemed to be a bit too giddy and immature, so I was demoted to the chorus to teach me a lesson. I didn't mind that as I was completely in love with the whole idea of being in a play and in an opera at that.

The following year I got the lead and the year after that as well and then my voice broke and I was told that I shouldn't sing to give my voice a rest and I was allowed to work backstage, painting and shifting scenery and working the lights and I was even more in love with the whole business. It was while I was a senior in the Jes that I played for the first time in a 'real' play in the Irish language theatre Taibhdhearc na Gaillimhe and from that out I was hooked on the theatre for the greater part of my life.

The teachers in the Jes were a mixed bunch consisting of three lay teachers in the lower school and the rest were either Jesuit priests or scholastics i.e. men who had not yet spent the required ten years of study.

The first of the lay teachers was a man called Waldron, who had been involved politically during the trouble times and as such was certain to get a job teaching in the Jes. He was never known by his correct name by the students but always as Leaper (pronounced Lipper). I have no idea why he got this name. He was of the old school that believed that education could be driven into small boys by punishment and terror and he spent much of his time shouting at us all as if we were deaf. To make a point he would bring a large stick, which was a roller from a wall map, crashing down on your desk with all of his might, accompanied by a stream of abuse and the certain knowledge that you were destined to be ignorant all of your life and begging on the streets. He wasn't much of a teacher.

The second lay teacher was Danny Griffin known affectionately by the boys just as Danny. He was the father of one of my contemporaries in the school, himself called Danny, who remains a friend to this day. Danny was a proper teacher, with proper qualifications and managed to get lots of information into our not too willing brains using wit and a certain forced sarcasm which appealed to us. His bon mot to us when we were leaving for the higher school was, "There ye go, I taught ye all I know and ye still know nothing."

The third of the lay teachers was known as 'Paorach' implying that he was somehow the chieftain of the Power clan. I'm not sure if he had been ever qualified as a teacher but I do know that he had been on the run during the civil war, which implied that he was a Republican. He had also fought in the Spanish civil war although I am not sure on which side. The fact that the Jes employed him might imply that he had fought for the Franco side, which used fighting for the Catholic Church as one of their reason for the war. Still he always wore a black Basque beret with a strange symbol on it that I can't remember but which would seem on recollection to be the symbol of the International Brigade.

He was our drill instructor and held the position that had been held by my grandfather some ten or fifteen years before this. He also taught us natural history and was a mine of information on wildlife; how to see them, care for them and indeed catch them. He loved the great outdoors and instilled a similar like in those of us who were prepared to listen to him.

The priests were a different proposition altogether and they varied greatly in their age, outlook and ability to teach. Father Fitzgibbon or 'Gibbo' taught us English at the lower level, in spite of the fact that he really despised English and would have preferred to teach Irish. He was also a talented musician and was in charge of one of the choirs, where he would teach us international songs that he had translated into Gaelic. One of these, which we used as a marching song in a youth movement known as *Guth Na nÓg*, was a wonderful translation of the German song *Erika*. Later we found out that this had also been the marching song of the German Panzer division and of the Hitler youth and it was quietly dropped.

Buggles or Fr. O'Kelly was our Maths teacher. He was a brilliant mathematician who spent his life dreaming up exotic formulae that he would spring on us the following morning. The problem was that he hadn't a clue how to teach and would give up in disgust when we were unable to understand what exactly he was trying to tell us with his equations and formulae. Outside of the school he was a kind and caring man who spent all of his spare time visiting the sick at home and in their hospital beds. Such was his popularity that Bishop Browne attempted to restrain him from these visits fearing that he was getting too friendly with the patients and that they might leave their money to him rather than to the bishop himself. I'm pleased to say the bishop's plan didn't work and he continued his good work right up to the end.

'Pateen' was Fr. Mallon who was the son of one of the executed IRA leaders of the 1916 rebellion and (naturally enough I suppose) he hated England and the English. He wore chrome rimmed spectacles and could use them as a rear view mirror to catch out boys who were paying less attention than he felt he deserved, upon which he would whirl and throw, with uncanny accuracy, a small piece of chalk at the offending boy. He was a talented musician who formed a small orchestra at the time in the city called Cáirde an Cheoil, or friends of music. He trained many of the boys in various instruments in their spare time who later went on to become classical players.

'Spits' was Fr. Michael O'Riley from Kerry who looked more as if he had come from India so sallow was his complexion. He was a peevish man with few social graces who attempted to teach us History and Geography, very badly in my opinion. He had a negative manner and was seldom inclined to inspire one to do the work but rather to complain about and deride our feeble efforts. As a result of his efforts and probably of my own lack of interest in his methods I came within inches of failing both of these subjects in my leaving certificate. The sad thing is that when I left school and delved into these subjects myself they became two of my abiding passions up until this day and I bemoan the fact that if I had been taught them properly I would have had a proper head start from a much earlier age.

There were very good teachers there as well such as Fr. Andy O'Reilly who taught us Latin with great vigour and humour and who was to become one of my great friends for the rest of his life. He was involved with the Columban Hall and was a great backstage man very adept at building sets for the school plays and at operating lighting and sound effects and I learned a lot from him of these skills as well as Latin.

Fr. O'Farrell taught us French and although very few of us actually got on with him, I found him to be a remarkable French teacher. He was a fanatic for the International Phonetic Code and made us scan a verse of poetry in this code every night, a task that would be impossible if one didn't know the pronunciation of the particular words. I was his best pupil so he was much harder on me than on anybody else, because he felt that I should know better what I was about. Later when I went to work in Paris in an office where nobody spoke any English my colleagues were surprised at my fluency but in particular at my pronunciation. He had a liver problem and we could tell in the morning by the colour of his face how the class was going to go for the rest of the day.

Fr. McGrath or 'Fatty' taught us English and was good at it. He was an intelligent man and outside of the school did wonderful work with the city's inner city boys with the Boys' Club of which he was the patron. He had a tendency to drift off sometimes in the afternoons after a long and tedious day and would come up with a start trying to find where it was he had left us before his reverie.

Fr. Eddie Divilly was a local boy and was one of the best teachers of Irish I ever had. He loved the language and everything about it and had a great ability to get on with the boys thereby instilling in them a love of the subject and a willingness to learn it. He too was the chief sports teacher and in particular the man who started rowing as a sport in the school, a sport with which he was to be associated, with tremendous enthusiasm, for the rest of his life. He too remained a friend of mine for many years until his death about five years ago.

There were other priests as well, perhaps another five or six who taught us, but who left not too deep an impression one way or another. The strange thing to reflect that nowadays there isn't a single priest teaching in the Jes and it is now a co-ed school – wouldn't we have loved that?

One of the highlights in our year at the Jes was the annual holiday trip to the Gaeltacht, or Irish speaking regions in the west of Ireland. Usually it was to Carraroe in Conamara, or on occasion to the Aran Islands. We were lucky when our turn came to be the ones to go to the Aran Islands. We stayed in Kilmurvy on Inis Mór in the famous home of the O'Flaherty Johnsons and spent the days talking Irish and playing games of rounders and swimming in the sea, which was about a hundred metres from our lodgings. What a summer that was and what fun we all had.

Two incidents stick in my mind from that summer; one was of huddling around the old battery radio listening to the news that war had just broken out in Korea and the other was the day the sharks came swimming with us.

News of the outbreak of war in Korea came through in late June 1950. There was great speculation on the day that this could be the start of world war three and when one considers that the Second World War had just finished some six or seven years before, I expect that this was not an unreasonable fear. We were glued to the radio for the next few days, worrying about what sort of war it would be if the two nuclear powers (USA and USSR) became actively involved.

Swimming with sharks is a different matter altogether. Now it should be said that the sharks in question were basking sharks or sometimes called sunfish, which are plankton feeders and pose no threat whatsoever to humans in the water. They are however very, very big, running to as much as twenty or thirty feet in length. In much of this sea area between the Aran and Achill islands they had been hunted almost to extinction for their livers, from which the oil was extracted, but the practice had been dying out by the time we were there.

As I mentioned, they posed absolutely no threat to us in the water, but to an impressionable teenager swimming about a hundreds yards offshore, when your pals on the beach begin screaming and jumping up and down and pointing behind you and you look about and see a series of dorsal fins heading your way in the water, believe me you do not hang about to see what species they are. There were about four or five of us, all strong swimmers, swimming together some distance offshore and as soon as we saw those dorsal fins we headed for the shore as fast as our various swimming techniques would let us. I would venture to say, that if somebody had put a stopwatch on us that day as we swam ashore, there is no doubt in my mind that we would have set the world record for teenage boys over the distance. Eventually the sharks got bored and went their way, but it was the following day before any of us would go back in the water.

Back at home, during the summers of those years life was pretty good and before the era of summer jobs we spent a lot of our time hanging out in the tennis club. Juniors were not allowed to play in the evenings so we would usually head up there after lunch and meet our mates, male and female, and play knockabout tennis. Sometimes if the weather was bad we would resort to the clubhouse and drag out the old wind-up gramophone, dust off the very limited and scratchy collection of records and hold impromptu dances. When tennis was finished we would hop on our bikes and cycle the short distance to Salthill to cool off with a swim and from there to the famous shop/café known as the Bon-Bon, where their ice cream sundaes were the perfect thing to top off the evening in the little ice cream parlour at the back of the shop. This was our equivalent of the American kids' drug store and we felt we were as sophisticated as any of the teenagers we saw in the American movies. Thinking back on this period in our lives I would venture to say that our lives were idyllic and without a care in the world.

I was happy enough at school and though I never quite covered myself in glory as a student I didn't attract too much abuse either and if we did get some sort of physical punishment from time to time, this was the norm in every school in those days.

Nowadays such teaching methods would have almost every teacher I ever had up in front of tribunals or in court for child abuse. Some people had it harder than others, but I think that mostly I got what I deserved under those rules, even though I was often indignant at the time.

11. Enjoying Life Afloat and in the Army

—⁓—

For me school years passed easily enough, particularly when I got to my senior years for it was then we started to get out in life and to do enjoyable things as a group. The first of these was rowing. For many years in Galway there had been a strong tradition of sports rowing but by the 1950s it was generally the preserve of the students of University College Galway and the members of the Galway Rowing Club who were recruited from various walks of life, many of them hardened manual workers. The idea of a schools rowing team was considered pretty far out, but it was decided to give it a go and our arch rivals, the Bish, and we were the first schools to participate.

An elderly dentist in the town called Anderson, who in his day had been a famous and dedicated oarsman, presented a trophy. The trophy, which bore his name, was to become the blue ribbon of schoolboy rowing in Ireland and is, as far as I know, still rowed for today. For the purposes of training we originally attached ourselves to the U.C.G. rowing club while the boys of the Bish became part of the Galway Rowing Club, thereby cementing the rivalry. In the beginning we used all College equipment from boats to oars and the Bish did the same with the G.R.C.

The big difference between us was that we used swivel style oars and boats, in which the oar is placed and locked into a swivel and this moves with the motion of the oar. The Bish and the G.R.C. used a much more antiquated and, some said, purist system that was known as block rowing in which the oar was placed between a couple of blocks of leather and metal and was freer to move about and also to come out under pressure.

Our training regime was brutal under the watchful eye of Fr. Eddie Divilly S.J. who was from Galway himself and steeped in the rowing tradition. We had to be togged out, ready to go at the U.C.G. boat club by seven in the morning and, having done our limbering-up exercises, climb into the boat and row at full tilt for Menlo graveyard which was about three miles upstream and against the current. All of this with a coxswain bellowing at us incessantly and our coach, using a megaphone in the follow up boat bellowing, "Watch that blade bow!", "Follow through two!", "C'mon stroke for God's sake will you pick it up!". There was no let up but drive, drive, drive, pull with all of your heart and get the timing so tight that all eight of you pulled at exactly the same split second and the boat seemed to fly through the water like some giant eight winged bird. It was brutally hard but it was equally exhilarating and when we reached Menlo graveyard, after catching our collective breaths, we had to go back down the river, doing the same thing again and maybe practicing a few starts along the way.

By the time we got back to the boathouse, we were well and truly exhausted. There was no let-up however as then we had to do two full laps of the old Galway Gaol buildings (now Galway Cathedral) and after a cold shower (there was no hot water), head home for breakfast and then in to school to be in time for classes, or face the slogs of the Prefect of Studies.

Needless to mention though that by the time the rowing season and the holidays came around we were well and truly fit and tough as old boots and we spent the best part of the summer going about the country to the various regattas in Athlone, Dublin, Cork,

Limerick, Portora Royal College in the North of Ireland, which we considered to be very toffee-nosed, and finally Carrick-on-Shannon which was the last regatta of the season. The first year we went to Portora, we saw in the programme that most of their crew had double barrelled names like Wutheringay-Smythe and McDermott-Carew and such, while we were described as Dick Byrne, Noel Carr and Brian Quigley, so we decided the next time we came we would also use our mothers maiden names so I became Clampett-Byrne and Noel became Prendergast-Carr while Brian became Hasset-Quigley. I don't think the Portora boys got it, or if they did they were far too polite to say so.

We liked Carrick for two reasons. First, it was the last regatta of the season and we were allowed to relax and let our hair down when it was over. The second reason was that Carrick-on-Shannon was home to one of the finest women's rowing clubs in the country that, more importantly, had a junior section. This junior section was also allowed to let their hair down at Carrick, especially at the Grand Regatta Ball that followed the last race and, well, suffice to say we usually let our hair down together.

Rowing was to be part of our lives for the next five or six years, even after school and when I left school, together with a few friends, we helped to revive rowing in the Corrib Rowing and Yachting Club. This was Galway's oldest club and a famous rowing club in the earlier part of the twentieth century, but it had allowed the rowing part of its title to die out and indeed the yachting part as well but that is another story.

Next to rowing, the most important thing to happen in those senior years was joining the army. I don't refer to the full-time regular army here, but to the Fórsa Cosanta Áitiúil, or F.C.A. (nicknamed the free clothing association) which had had the earlier name of the L.D.F. or Local Defence Force. This was the equivalent of the Territorial Army in Britain, or the Army Reserve in the US. There had been a fall off in the recruitment to this force in the years following the war until somebody got the bright idea that it would be good to recruit young fellows from the local schools who would be reasonably intelligent and enthusiastic for the adventure of playing soldiers.

The Jes was the first to be recruited, followed closely by the Bish and although there was still great rivalry between the schools we were all now serving together in A Company of the 50th Battalion and pounding the same drill square of Renmore Barracks which my grandfather's regiment, the Connacht Rangers, had been pounding only about thirty years previously.

Sergeants and sergeant majors shouted at us, corporals shouted at us, officers shouted at us and it seemed that it was impossible for anybody to do anything in the army unless somebody was walking beside them bellowing in their ears. We soon got the idea though and it wasn't long until we were parading and drilling with the same skill and precision as the regular army. In fact it was said that following our basic training in foot and rifle drill we were considerably more jildi (an army word possibly of Indian origin for being smart and meticulously turned out and precise in detail) than our regular army colleagues. When a visiting dignitary came to town, such as the President of Ireland or a high ranking government minister, or senior church leader, we were the boys they brought out to present the guard of honour and we learned all the tricks for impressing the natives, such as polishing our bayonets with Brasso so they really did glint in the sun and boning oxblood polish into our boots before polishing them so that they shone like glass. There was also a trick of slightly unlocking the magazine on our Lee Enfield rifles so that when you presented arms and slapped them back in there was an audible clatter, which, if you got it together, was most impressive.

Young men and guns are a heady combination and as well as flinging them about our bodies in our arms drill we also learned how to actually shoot with them. The principle weapon used was the ubiquitous Short Magazine Lee Enfield rifle known as 'Smelly' by the First World War Tommys because of the initials. The weapons we used had all seen service in the British army before passing on to the Irish army and they bore the broad arrow of the British ordnance office. The weapon itself had been the principle rifle used all through the First and Second World Wars by the British army and was probably one of the finest rifles ever developed. If you were good, it was possible to get six well-aimed shots off in about forty seconds and if the rifle had been well zeroed by a decent armourer, a skilful marksman could put all of these shots into a circle the size of a man's chest at up to three hundred yards.

Not many of us had these skills however and some of our number could hardly hit a target no matter how near it was. I was a fair to middling shot and qualified for my marksman's badge and on a good day, if I concentrated, I could get half of my shots in the inner circle and the rest not too far away. One of our colleagues, though not a member of our school group, was a dead shot and I recall an incident in which one of the company, unwilling to drink tea out of army-issue tin mugs, had brought in his own white china one and left it standing on the one-hundred-yard range when we moved back to the three-hundred-yard. It sat there very conspicuously and glinted in the sun and was a sorely tempting target. Word came down the line for everybody to fire a wide shot this time so that the culprit could not be determined and when the order to fire came the mug flew up into the air and shattered into a thousand pieces accompanied by a loud cheer. It was an astonishing shot and although the duty officer called an immediate investigation, it was found that nobody had actually hit a target at all on that occasion. While it may now be regarded as a puerile exercise we were only young lads and nobody got hurt except the pride of he who wouldn't use an army mug.

At a certain time of the year usually in the late summer we were all sent off to military camp. In our case it was usually to Finner Camp within a mile or so of Bundoran in County Donegal. This was a great occasion for us and one that we greatly enjoyed. In the first instance, we got a cash grant of twenty pounds for the fortnight, which was a serious amount of money in those days (a manual worker would have been doing well to earn it in a month). Not only that but we had free accommodation, such as it was, and free food. In return we were expected to do our share of square bashing, rifle firing on the range and other exotica such as the use of hand and rifle grenades.

Our accommodation consisted of semi-circular sectioned Nissan huts made of corrugated iron and lined with timber sheeting. Each hut held about twenty bunks with a couple of solid fuel stoves in the centre. Each man had a box into which he would put his gear and a wardrobe-like hanging area in which to hang his clothes. On arrival everybody was issued with a tin plate, a bowl-like dish, a mug, knife, fork and spoon. This was your kit and you were expected to hand it all back again clean and in good order at the end of your stay, or pay a fine for any part that was missing.

The food was wholesome and plentiful and though cooked to within an inch of its life was also fairly palatable, except for two days, one at the beginning of the camp and one at the end. These were the days when the army instructed the cooks to include a liberal dose of jollop (the army term for a laxative or purgative). The theory was that since most of the men who turned up came from different backgrounds, some city and some rural, it was necessary to purge them of what their stomachs contained before embarking on a steady diet of army food and again, having finished the camp, before returning home.

The effect of the jollop, which could be concealed in anything from the soup to the dessert, was to ensure that every man spent about three hours in the bogs moaning as if his life was ending. Some of the wide boys, one of my mates included, discovered that if you dropped the few bob to whoever was kitchen orderly on the day, he would brief you as to which course contained the dreaded purgative and you could simply leave that behind on your plate. This was well worth the investment and worked like a charm, especially when we were free to go to town in our civvies to meet the local and tourist belles at the famous Astoria Ballroom while our colleagues were crapping the night away in the blocks of dry latrines.

It was on one of these early visits to town that we had one of our lucky breaks. Because of the absence of hot water for shaving at the camp, a buddy of mine from Roscommon and myself hit on the bright idea that we would come in to town early, get our tickets and go into the Astoria Ballroom which had a plentiful supply of hot water which meant to us that we could shave there in comfort. Having attended to our ablutions we could then head out into the town for an hour or two before returning to the dance. On this particular night I had had my shave and was indulging in a comfortable session in the toilet, when I reached up to what I took to be a bundle of toilet paper on the windowsill only to discover that it was, in fact, a large bundle of money amounting to hundreds of pounds. Having finally got my mate to shove some real toilet paper in under the door, I finished my business and we took the large bundle with us to the guy in the dress suit who guarded the door. We made some smart remark about it being a bit too valuable to use as toilet paper and asked him for a receipt just in case. Having done this we headed out on the town to enjoy the heady delights of the local fun fair and the rifle range, where with our finely honed rifle skills we often won some furry toy or other. As we returned to the ballroom the guy on the door asked us to hold on and he went and got the manager, who confided in us that the money we had found had been the previous night's takings which he had absentmindedly left on the window sill and later assumed to have been stolen. He had been in a complete state of panic all day the poor man, so when he came on duty he was, to say the least of it, considerably relieved. The upshot of our little civic act was that he gave us free access to the whole place and all of its facilities for the remainder of our holiday, for ourselves and our partners of choice. All in all it was a good result and we certainly enjoyed the remainder of our stay that year.

As we got older we had the option of what camps and courses we would take in Finner and there would be N.C.O.s or officer's training courses and specialist courses on the Bren gun or on the Gusted sub-machine gun and other complicated stuff. Usually late in the summer around August there would just be basic courses that didn't require any hard work or studying. These were the favourite courses for laid-back soldiers like me, especially since this was the time that the Scottish factory girls would descend on Bundoran every year, so we would try to dodge until these courses if we could.

These girls were unlike anything we had ever experienced before, as most of the girls we knew were secondary school girls who had been terrorised by the nuns into believing that if you even held a man's hand too close you might become pregnant and it was a mortal sin. The Scottish girls didn't appear to have any concept of sin and were hell bent on enjoying themselves day and night for their holidays and we were only too eager to oblige.

The year that I succeeded in dodging any courses was, I think, my last year in the force and those in command had realised what we were up to and so decided that this would be the camp at which the place would be cleaned and tidied up. On our first day we were surprised to be lined up by our sergeant major who began by saying, "We realise that you fellas have come here to doss, but we are wise to ye and now I'm going to be calling for volunteers and when I do you better step forward smartish." He then called for farmers' sons and three unfortunates stepped forward. He instructed them to go to the quartermaster and get their equipment, which turned out to be shovels, and they were sent to dig out a new long trench for the next latrine and made to fill in the old one. He then called for builders' sons and they were sent to assist in the moving of the same toilets. He continued in this vein until the line was getting smaller and I became more worried until he called for an artist. Since I did a bit of painting and fancied that this would be easier than the preceding jobs I stepped forward and was sent to the quartermaster's store where I was handed a large can of black paint and two brushes, one large and one small. I was then told to go and paint the stoves in all of the barracks, which numbered about twenty-five, with two stoves to the billet. I am pleased to say I had a most relaxing week painting those stoves at a leisurely pace. The following week I was teaching new recruits how to shoot, which was a bit more frenetic. Our nights were filled with Scottish girls and dancing and riding in the amusement park – life was good.

I spent the statutory period of five years in the army and left with an honourable discharge to do other things when my time was up.

Many of my colleagues however went on to become life members of the F.C.A. and ended up being some of the most senior officers in the force. It is interesting that the camaraderie that was begun back in those days still surfaces whenever I meet one of my old army colleagues and the talk always turns to the fun and games and to how much we all enjoyed that particular time in our lives. I still feel that the discipline and sense of duty that was given to us all back then during that period of army life has stood to us all throughout our lives and I sometimes think that the youth of today are really missing out on a wonderful opportunity by not joining in greater numbers. Of course some of them still do and I'm sure it benefits them enormously.

12. Bringing Light to the Nation

—⚡—

We have by now reached the early nineteen fifties, which, like the previous thirty years, was a time of serious depression in the land. Many of my boyhood friends, at this stage of their lives, found themselves with little choice but to board the mail boat for England or, if they could afford it, the liner for America for there were very, very few jobs to be had in our part of Ireland, or indeed in any part of Ireland for that matter. Europe was still licking its not inconsiderable wounds following the war and Ireland, which had stood aloof from participating in that great conflict, found herself cut adrift economically from the rest of the world. In those days not many of my contemporaries managed to get to university and even those who did were still forced in the most part to go away to find work.

During my last year at school I had got a summer job, courtesy of my father's contacts, as a part-time employee of the E.S.B. (Electricity Supply Board) in Galway City, working in the stores and sometimes operating the telephone switchboard, which really wasn't much of a task in those days as all of the telephones in Galway only had two digits. For example the E.S.B, which had three lines, was Galway 21, 22 and 23. The County Council was 35 and so on. I enjoyed the work and more to the point I got on well with most of the people working there.

So following my leaving cert, in which I didn't exactly cover myself in glory, but managed to scrape through, I found myself looking for a full-time job and though I managed to attend U.C.G. many, many years later, at that time I didn't have the wherewithal to become a full time student. My forte was drawing and when the E.S.B. advertised that they were looking for a trainee draughtsman, I applied. Possibly because I was known, or out of respect for my dad, or maybe because I was one of only two boys who had actually sat Drawing in the leaving certificate in the whole city, I landed the job. I was now out in the real world with the responsibility of looking after myself and earning real money and leaving my childhood days behind forever.

Under the watchful eye and guidance of a man called Dick Kilgariff, who ran the drawing office I was quickly trained and brought up to speed on the business of drawing, surveying and plotting E.S.B lines on to ordinance maps, just ready to be deployed in to a rural electrification gang.

At this time the rural electrification of Ireland was just underway and the plan was to have the entire country connected to the national electricity grid, no matter how remote or sparsely inhabited. It was a huge undertaking and to put it in the correct context, the rural electrification of Great Britain had not yet begun at this time. We didn't think about it too deeply at the time but we were probably building what was to become the most important piece of infrastructure for the future development of the country and the networks we laid down back then have changed little since that time.

To explain the process there is a need for some tedious detail, but I will make it as brief as possible. To electrify a rural area it was necessary firstly to survey the area, on ordinance maps and then on the ground to determine in which direction the power supply should come to the particular area and having done that plot the lines of high tension poles and connected to them the number of low tension poles needed to bring the actual electricity into the individual houses.

When the survey was complete, it was necessary for the map man, me in this instance, to go and mark out the location of every single pole using marked and numbered timber pegs, which were driven into the ground and then marked on a separate map. Behind me came the pole man, in our gang sometimes called the horseman, Mike Heneghan, who with a horse and chain dragged the particular pole from the nearest pole dump beside the road in through the various fields only to leave it beside the particular peg for which it was intended. If the going were particularly tough, the tractor man Mick Bourke would carry out this job. The digging gang then came and dug the holes by hand in the old fashioned way with a pick and shovel (The J.C.B. and the mechanical hole-borers had not yet arrived back in those days). These holes were about two metres deep and about a metre square. When the holes were ready the poles were erected, again by a specialist team who had a sort of wigwam device, which had been invented by one of their number to raise the pole and drop it into the hole. Following that, it was plumbed to ensure that it was straight and when this had been done the wiring gang came and strung the wires from pole to pole and from the nearest pole to the various houses along the route.

The whole thing was very well rehearsed and in general went like clockwork. Of course in those days there was no such thing as danger money or wet time or snow time so this work had to be achieved whatever the weather and in our case in some of the most exposed and remote parts of this island. I recall working in about half a metre of snow in an area called Doon near Westport, helping the crew to locate some pegs I had driven in only a couple of weeks beforehand, but which were now buried without a trace. When they were found eventually, the ground had to be dug snow or no snow.

If one were to draw a comparison with any other form of grouping of men, I expect that the E.S.B. gang came very close to being an army platoon, with its own specialists and rankings. The group engineer was the commander of the team and took full responsibility for the overseeing of every aspect of the job and was only answerable to high command, which in our case was the District Engineer who hailed from Cork and was called McCarthy. The first lieutenant was the area organiser; a man who had the job of making sure that everybody in the area took the option of having electricity installed. The second lieutenants were the clerks, who had the responsibility of ordering everything we required, checking its arrival and paying the men and myself, whose duties I have already outlined. The N.C.O.s were the foreman and the various gangers, while the rank and file were the men who actually did the digging and the hoisting and the wiring.

Having a job of any kind in any part of Ireland in those difficult cash-strapped post-war days was considered to be the height of fortune and good luck, but for country lads, many of them the sons of small and at the time, poor, farmers, to have a job in the E.S.B. was a benefit beyond measure, for it separated them from many of their peers by keeping them off the emigrant ship and allowing them to work not too far from home and bring home a reasonable wage packet at the end of each week. They were a happy-go-lucky bunch and, with very few exceptions, worked cheerfully at whatever task they were given. Of course because of their apparent solvency it made them very, very acceptable as potential husbands, but more about that later.

My first appointment came when I was dropped off at the side of the road with my suitcase and large two-cross-barred bicycle about seven miles from my destination, Tourmakeady, by the district foreman Harry Wall, with the exhortation to be sure to write to my mother, keep well clear of the Mayo women and, for the love of God, if I felt the urge to start writing poetry to head for home. With that he left me in a cloud of dust and exhaust fumes. A sort of unimaginable silence fell over the location and me.

Here I was a young lad from the city, known then amongst the gang as a townie, who was used to being never more than a few feet from some sort of noise or other, listening for any sort of sound, but only hearing the occasional distant cawing of some crows. I loaded up my bag and my gear, which consisted of a theodolite and a couple of ranging rods strapped to the crossbars and I struck out on my official span-new bike heading for the local office, which was sited in Derrig's pub in Tourmakeady. It was common enough for pubs to accommodate the local E.S.B. office for usually they had spare sheds out behind which could be converted into stores and offices. They also had toilets which were considered necessary for the office staff and also most of them, even back in those days, were equipped with telephones, with which they ordered their supplies and which our staff could use for keeping in touch with head office.

Getting about meant cycling the enormous bike up hills and down dales in the face of wind and rain or in the boiling sun and I can say that at that time I was fitter than I have ever been before or since. In the morning I would check with the engineer regarding the next area or group to be electrified and loading up my trusty bike with pegs, a hammer and the theodolite I would head off for the day to find the area and to peg it out, taking particular care to number each peg so that it could be identified later by the pole gang who would make sure that the correct size of pole was erected in that location.

Having driven the peg I would then mark it on a copy of the map and fill out a way-leave form, which had then to be presented to the owner of the land in question. Some of them were quite agreeable, as they knew that arrival of the electricity was, at this stage, almost inevitable and for their own benefit. Some, however were not so welcoming and in my time I had dogs set on me and shotguns pointed at me and every sort of verbal abuse imaginable shouted at me, but it was my job to hand over the way-leave and if given the opportunity to explain it to them, pointing out that they had seven days to complain officially in writing to the district office. Very few of them ever did, although some of them took the law into their own hands. Apocryphal tales abounded of men who went out in the night and cut down the poles that had been recently erected. Of course this only meant that the Garda were called in and that new poles were put back and the man who cut them down had to pay for the cost of the renewal out of his own pocket. One farmer put his son down in a hole and left him there for an entire day to prevent the E.S.B. lads from erecting the pole, knowing that if they touched his son it would technically be an assault. Eventually a compromise was reached and as far as I know, the entire affair ended amicably. I remember on one occasion telling a lady farmer that the pole in her haggard would be no more dangerous than a tree. "In that case," she said, "I don't want it there at all, for a tree was struck by lightening here a couple of years ago and two of my cows got killed under it." I never used that bright idea again.

For me, living in the country was a totally new experience. True I had lived in Westport in my grandparents house and forayed out into the country and had spent an odd week on a cousin's farm when I was about eight or nine, but here I was, for the foreseeable future, a slick townie, used to going to the pictures and to dances on a regular basis and used to listening to the radio and my records in the evenings at home. Out here there was no electricity while we were there and as a result very, very few radios. If one came upon a device for playing records it was inevitably something with a large brass horn on it and a handle that had to be wound vigorously before producing scratchy and pretty feeble sound. The only light in my digs was a series of oil-filled lamps with wicks and, when going to bed, a candle. For entertainment we usually sat around the open fire, listening to and telling stories. In some houses cards were played, usually a game called twenty-fives.

In Tourmakeady, which is where I was first stationed, a well-known visiting house was Durkan's, which was also the post office and it was often common for anything up to nine or ten people, including the family and friends to be gathered around their fireplace at night singing songs or telling stories on just hanging about. The fact that there were a couple of personable young girls in the house helped to bring out the swains such as myself. In the winter this helped to assuage any loneliness that I might have had being away from home and on my own. Durkan's was a great house for storytelling and it was common for the older generation to tell yarns of times not long gone during the troubles and the struggle for Irish freedom.

Not far from the house was the entrance to Tourmakeady House, later to become the residence of English film actor Robert Shaw, but more famous locally at that time as the scene of an ambush in which members of the R.I.C. were killed during the troubles. One of the favourite stories told was how this particular area was supposed to be haunted by the ghosts of the unfortunate victims and many were the tales of people's hair going white overnight with the fear, having encountered the same spirits. I would feel that somehow spirits of another sort may have been the real reason for such reported sightings, but as an impressionable young man not long in a country area, these stories left me with not a little apprehension, especially since I had to walk by this particular entrance gate on my way home from the storytelling sessions in pitch dark in the dead of night.

The area was very heavily wooded and the trees formed a canopy across the whole road; even on fairly bright nights such was the cover overhead that it was not possible to see the hands, literally, in front of your face. One night as I was going home after a particular spooky session, whistling to myself to allay my nervousness, I nearly dropped dead when a voice, seemingly within a foot of my face, spoke to me. I got such a fright that I didn't understand what had been said and I asked him to repeat. It was then I discovered that the man was speaking in Irish and merely asking me for a light for his cigarette. Still shaking I took the box of matches out of my pocket and I could hear them rattling as I tried to open the box and light one. Eventually I succeeded and in the light of the match I recognised a local man whom I knew fairly well to see holding his face towards me with a cigarette in his mouth and his hands cupped around it. I lit his cigarette and with some pleasantry or other walked on home trying to act nonchalant, but it was a hundred metres or more before my heart stopped pounding and my knees stopped shaking. It was a while before I walked home late on my own again and I got into the habit of bringing my E.S.B. torch with me.

Of course the poor man had been wearing Wellingtons that made his footsteps inaudible to me and dying for a smoke, he couldn't believe his luck when he heard me coming and saw the glow of my cigarette. I'm sure he thought that I was a little curt on that occasion but he wasn't to know that he had scared the pants off me.

13. Life on the 'Rural'

It is quite remarkable sometimes how the human mind and body can adapt to changed situations and it wasn't long before I found that I had settled in quite comfortably to the rural life. I had been brought up in the city where the radio, electric light, the electric kettle and hot water were taken for granted, where hot meals could be served up straight out of the electric or gas oven and where washing machines, though not universal, were beginning to become the standard labour-saving devices for the housewives in the cities and towns. (In those years it was still permissible to call them housewives for that is what the great majority of them were and proud of it.)

The lives of their country counterparts couldn't have been more different. Hot water if required had to be boiled in a great basin or pot on the open fire, the same fire upon which the dinner had to be cooked. Washing machines were non-existent here; a large zinc oval bath or basin with two handles for transporting it and hanging it on the wall when not in use was the clothes-washing device. It was also the place in which children were bathed and in which adults, not having any showers or proper indoor bathrooms, washed themselves at the weekend.

In the place that I had my digs, water for washing or cooking had to be brought in a bucket from a deep well situated about thirty metres from the back door of the house. If there was much activity in the house this bucket, which held about two gallons and weighed about sixteen pounds or a stone when full, had to be filled and carried several times a day and this job fell to the women of the house, either the mother or her eighteen year old daughter. The men of the house, father and son, both called Alfie, were working for the E.S.B. as casual labourers for the duration of the job in their neighbourhood, as well as working their little farm, while myself and my fellow lodger, a Scottish lad called Jim, helped out when we could, but were almost always out for most of every day. The house was considered to be very lucky as they had two members of the family getting wages every week and two lodgers who paid them the princely sum of around two pounds each bed and board, which back in those lean early fifties was considered to be a fair sum of money indeed.

If I could wrangle a lift, I would go home for the weekend, but more often than not we spent the weekends in Tourmakeady as well. The highlight of the weekend was a dance held in the Parish Hall. This was watched over very carefully by the local parish priest who had very strong ideas concerning the coming together of young people of opposite sexes and watched the dance floor with a hawk-like eye to make sure that the young women of the parish were not going to be corrupted by the young men, especially these new blow-ins from the E.S.B. who had a reputation for being hard men in every way. If you got too close to one of the girls and actually had two arms about her in the slow dances he would come over and fix you with a stare. If you didn't get the message he would call the girl away and give her a talking to. As it was, the band was encouraged not to play too many slow dances and ceili type dances were the preferred dance where all of the dancers were in long lines and only got together for the 'house' or swing at the end of each section.

Another device operated by the priest was the positioning of a Tilley paraffin lamp outside the hall on a hook to make sure that no young men left the hall with young women. Of course the young men and women were alert to his plan and would go off together in same-sex groups only to meet up with the opposite sex outside the range of the Tilley lamp. They were, after all, normal boys and girls who wanted to do the normal things that young men and women did and were not overly impressed with the parish priest's efforts. I often felt at the time that it would have been smarter for the parish priest to allow them to leave the hall together, for in that way he might have had some idea of who was going out with whom, instead of having the whole business treated like some cloak and dagger mystery. Times were different then and parish priests had terrible powers.

It is to be remembered that these were still the days in which a young woman, if she became pregnant without a husband might well find herself condemned to slave like a prisoner in the nearest Magdalen Laundry for the rest of her life, have her baby taken from her by the Mercy Sisters and raised until it was old enough to be placed for adoption here or abroad without any recourse to the law or justice. All of this could and did happen on a nod from the local parish priest to prevent scandal and to stop the unfortunate girl from becoming an occasion of sin to the parish. The guilty man, if he wished to remain anonymous, walked free of responsibility or apparent stain on his character.

Around this time an organisation called Gaeltarra Éireann was set up to give employment in Gaelic-speaking remote rural areas. This was, in many respects, a terrific idea for the remote parts of Ireland at that time were not only employment black spots, but also black holes where no work of any sort was available. The people at Gaeltarra Éireann targeted the young women of these areas and set up factories in which they could be employed making items that would be readily saleable. In Tourmakeady, the factory, which employed anything up to a hundred young women, was engaged in knitting Aran sweaters and other similar types of traditional clothing. It was a great success and ensured that many young women could stay at home and get a weekly wage. The problem was that not enough thought was given to employing young men and they were still forced to emigrate, leaving the area devoid of solvent young men who might have been husband material for these girls, for in those far off days, it was still the hope and aim of most young people that one day they might be able to marry and have families.

It was a pity that people who had dreamed up the idea of giving employment to these country girls didn't find similar schemes or give assistance to a like number of young farmers' sons so that they might have been able to avoid the emigrant boat and start young Irish families which would have given strength to the rural economy when it was most needed.

Instead of this, the area had now many girls and apart from the visiting E.S.B. crew, hardly any indigenous males, most of whom had left on the boat for England or America to seek out employment.

Of course this was good for the single E.S.B. lads and many of them struck up relationships with these young women, only to be forced to leave them again when the area was completed and they had to move on.

Now and again, if the van could be borrowed, or enough people mustered to afford a taxi we would head for the dizzying heights of Westport to hear a real band play and dance real dances the way we wanted too, arriving back at all hours of the morning exhausted but happy. Sometimes we would go to Ballinrobe or Westport to go to the pictures and get a bag of fish and chips afterwards before heading back to base. These excursions were usually taken in very crowded taxis, which in those days were inevitably large American saloon cars such as Ford V8s, Dodges or Chevys. In a pinch they could hold six or seven slightly squeezed passengers and often did.

When I could get back to Galway for the weekends I would hang out with my mates, two of whom were medical students and identical twin brothers. Their father bought them a fine old flat-nosed Morris Oxford convertible doctor's coupé with a Dickie seat in the back. The problem the boys had of course was that they never had any money with which to buy petrol and keep up their student lifestyles at the same time. This was where I came in. Since I was making good money, I could fill the car and make use of it for the weekend and that would leave them with enough petrol to operate it until I came back again the following week. I was happy with the arrangement and so were they, particularly since we all hung out together in the first place and as likely as not they would be with me while driving about in the old car, so they gained a driver and I got the use of the car, which in the early fifties was part of every young man's dream. One night the car was parked outside their digs in lower Salthill and we were all inside the house listening to some records, when an almighty crash sounded outside. We ran out to find that a local shopkeeper from Salthill, known for his inability to drive after consuming the odd bottle of whisky, had crossed the road in his fairly modern Ford 100E Prefect, going at about forty miles per hour and had slammed head on into the old Morris Oxford, which had spring metal front bumpers. This combined with a less than beefy handbrake, meant that the Oxford retreated about two metres under the head-on impact with no visible damage, while the Ford was reduced to a twisted pile of its component parts containing the remarkably undamaged shop keeper who was fast asleep behind the remains of the wheel. The police duly arrived as did the emergency services and it was generally agreed that it was the weakish handbrake on the Morris Oxford that saved his life by allowing the car to reverse and absorb most of the energy of the impact. My first car crash and we weren't even in the car. It did however give us a good demonstration of the strength of the older car in comparison to the modern less robust car and a good idea of what can happen if you drive after consuming a bottle of whisky. Lessons were learned that evening.

It was sometime after this that I purchased my own first vehicle. The vehicle in question was purchased from one of my mates, Sinclair Kenny, and was a barely roadworthy Rudge Ulster motorbike. I say it was barely roadworthy when really I should say road legal, since it was a racing motorcycle which had previously belonged to Reg Kavanagh, the Irish motorcycle ace, and it had neither mudguards nor lights and because the compression was so high, it could not be kick started, but had to be run started in the manner of the Pony Express riders of our favourite movies, by running alongside and then jumping astride when it fired into life. I paid eight pounds for this beast and the fee included being able to leave it in Sinclair's father's domestic garage, which was only about two hundred yards from our house. This was an important part of the deal since if my father knew that I had sat on a motorbike, let alone owned one, there would have been serious ructions in our house. Although my father had previously driven a large Indian motorbike in the course of his work, he had a very serious respect for them and would have had a great fear that his only child might be reduced to an ex child and also probably would have killed me himself in the process of letting me know of this fear.

So I now had independence in getting to and from work in Mayo and could be sure that I would be able to get home every weekend if I wanted to. The drill was that I would go down to the Kenny's garage to which I now had a key at about six o clock on the Monday morning and wheel out the bike and drive like the wind to my job in Mayo; a distance of about fifty miles and arrive in time to start work at eight o'clock.

To say that this was a dangerous game was putting it lightly, for not alone was the machine far too fast for an inexperienced biker such as myself, but the fact that my father did not know that I had it was almost certain to cause serious retribution, because though I felt myself to be an adult, I was almost certain to incur his wrath and, though a quiet man, like a sleeping guard dog, one did not poke him with a stick. I kept it up for about a year and became unseated a couple of times though not doing any serious physical damage on any occasion, except almost joining a corpse in a coffin one day while speeding down Quay Hill in Westport only to meet a large funeral coming in the opposite direction with wall to wall people and my great aunt's husband, Pat Kerins who was a sergeant in the Garda, in the van. With more luck than skill I managed to stop and having had a serious lecture from Pat I decided it was time to end my motorcycle career. I sold the monster back to Sinclair

Kenny for almost the same price I had paid for it. It was some time again before I became the owner of mechanised transport.

As mentioned earlier in this chapter, dancing was the prime entertainment for us all and there were plenty of dance halls in the neighbourhood and in those days plenty of terrific bands as well. This was some time before the era of the show bands and many of the big bands styled themselves orchestras. In this part of Mayo there was the Brose Walsh orchestra, which actually had their own ballroom in Ballyheane. From Castlebar there was the Stephen Garvey orchestra, with whom my mother had actually played piano in her earlier days. Of course there were national bands as well that toured the country playing at dances from North to South. The most famous of these for a while was Mick Delahunty, who hailed from the South of Ireland and Maurice Mulcahy from Cork, but these were knocked into the shade with the arrival of the Hugh Toorish Band, commonly called The Clipper Carlton.

The Clipper Carlton hailed from Strabane in the North of Ireland and was, in every sense of the words, the first and best showband to arrive in Ireland or any place else for that matter. It consisted of a group of multi-instrumentalists, who could also sing dance and put on a vaudeville show at the same time. They were terrific and within a year or so had dancehall revellers eating out of their hands wherever they went. Everybody wanted to see and hear them and they filled houses at every venue.

I had first heard of them from a penpal of mine from Sligo, who used to enthuse about Hugh Toorish and his band in almost every letter she wrote. My turn to hear them came when I was stationed in Westport with the E.S.B. As it happened, on the night I was there before the dance started, so as not to miss anything of their performance, when Hugo Quinn, their trumpeter and one of the lead singers, was warming up a valve spring broke in his cornet and it couldn't be played. I was, at the time, a member of the Westport Brass Band and without further ado we hopped into the Clipper's bus and headed for the band hall, where I presented him with several cornets to try out. In the end he opted to take a valve spring out of an old battered instrument and use it in his own and the night was saved. Hugo and I were now buddies. In fact this friendship was to last for many a year as myself and some of my mates who had a band in Galway got the relief band gig from the proprietors of the Hangar (Pavilion) Ballroom in Galway and got to play relief for the Clippers every time they came to town, but more about that later.

Dancing was without a doubt the main entertainment for most of the youth of Ireland at this time and even though all of the ballrooms in the country were 'dry' (alcohol free) houses it didn't matter since most of the youth, male or female didn't drink and those who did usually were satisfied with a pint or two, since it wasn't considered nice to have the smell of drink on your breath when dancing with a young woman in those days and it might actually cause her to refuse to dance with you. I didn't drink back then so that was not a problem.

The drill was if you met up with some young woman you knew or fancied you danced with her and eventually would invite her to have a mineral (a soda in American talk), which in those days was a fizzy orange or lemon drink, as Coca Cola or Pepsi had not yet arrived and were unknown in Ireland. There was a hope that if she went with you, she at least liked you enough to talk to you and who knew, if you played your cards right, danced with her a few more times, if you weren't too much of a bore she might be persuaded to allow you to walk or cycle her home, since motorcars were few and far between amongst our dancing community. Inevitably this might also mean walking her sister or her cousin or her friend home as well, for even though promiscuity was virtually unknown in those days, most young women took no chances. If you succeeded in finally getting her on her own, there might be a chance of a bit of a 'court' before she went in, which meant that you might have exchanged a few kisses and hugs before you left to walk home alone. While this may seem very tame and unrewarding to modern youth, this was the way of things in those days and anybody who went any further than that was considered to be fast and was to be watched carefully.

There were apocryphal tales of boys and or girls who were known to go 'the whole way' but one seldom met anybody who could verify such tales.

But I digress, when the girls had been seen home and bade their farewells and kissed goodnight, it would be time to have a bag of greasy chips at the nearest outlet, usually a battered caravan or truck with smoke billowing from it at or near the dancehall, before piling into the taxi and heading home in the early hours of the morning, tired but happy and ready for another day's work the following day.

When all of the pegging and hole-digging and pole-erection and wire-stringing had been completed throughout the area and all of the houses connected to the still dormant local grid, the news would come that the 'switch-on' was to take place. Before this the demonstration unit would arrive. This consisted of a giant truck and trailer known as a Tasker trailer after its inventor. The trailer would be crammed with all sort of electrical devices from cookers to water pumps and toasters to electric kettles. The local demonstrator, usually a lady with a diploma or a degree in domestic economy, would arrive and begin baking and cooking with the power of a generator and when the time came for the demonstrations she would have cakes, bread and cooked chickens ready for people to taste as she explained the benefits of clean efficient electric power to the assembled locals, usually the women. At a given signal on the great day some local politician or religious leader would be asked to throw the switch and to great applause would do so and the whole place would light up. Of course they weren't to know that not far away up on a pole someplace the local electrician had just thrown the real switch to make this possible.

In the time that I spent with the E.S.B. rural gang from 1953 to 1955 we were responsible for electrifying all or most of South Mayo in a line from Westport to Castlebar and down to below Ballinrobe and the Galway border and most of North Galway in and about the Tuam, Glenamaddy, Dunmore area. It was a tremendous achievement, carried out by dedicated men who knew what they were doing and who got on with it no matter what the weather or the conditions, without danger money, wet day money or time off for snow or gales. The system worked and worked well and there were no protestors of any hue trying to stop the work, or objecting to poles or lines across the countryside, or wondering what effect they would have on the environment.

What they did achieve was phenomenal and in one single swoop they brought all of rural Ireland from a backward, eighteenth or nineteenth century lifestyle, cooking in pots over an open fire and trimming the wicks on oil lamps into the relative comfort of the twentieth century with light and power and communication. I doubt greatly if it could have been achieved today, as the many self-appointed guardians of the environment as well as the eco warriors, luddites and NIMBYs would have objected to the works every inch of the way.

Was it worth it? Of course it was. Would I do it all again? More than likely since, hard as it was, it was a job and half decent jobs were extremely rare in those days, especially ones that would pay you a living wage.

14. Back in Galway

—⚮—

While I had enjoyed my time with the E.S.B. and made many friends and accumulated many great life-forming experiences, one of my life's ambitions was to become involved in architecture; a subject that had fascinated me for much of my life.

One of my best friends from school and after, Noel Dowley had shared my ambition and he had gone on to serve his time as a draughtsman with Ed. Ralph Ryan Architects and Engineers, which was then the biggest office in Galway. It was there he met Simon J. Kelly, a fairly recently qualified architect from Westport. In 1955 Simon J. or Seán, as we knew him, decided that he wanted to open an architectural office of his own in Galway and Noel left to join him. They established the company Simon J. Kelly and Co. Architects in Eyre Square in Galway late in 1954 and by mid 1955 they were on the lookout for another draughtsman apprentice. This was just the opportunity I had looked for although it meant dropping from a weekly salary of around eight pounds, to one pound and ten shillings. However, I would be living at home and by having a bit of a dance band with some other friends I was able to supplement this by a few extra pounds per week. There was no contest as far as I was concerned and I jumped at the chance to begin my career in architecture, with which I would earn my living for almost the next fifty years.

Simon Kelly's was unlike any place I had ever worked before. The office was smaller with only about four people working there including Simon himself and the atmosphere was much more laid back and casual than I had been used to. We spent a fair bit of time on the drawing boards, mostly working on church buildings and we did a lot of laughing. Since I could drive I was also given the task of surveying sites and buildings on which we were working. For me it was an amazing experience; being paid to do what I really loved doing and most of the time I went to work with a smile on my face.

Simon had landed the job as diocesan architect and in these fairly lean years the Catholic Church was one of the few organisations which could afford to hire architects and build new churches, as well as repair the existing nineteenth century stock of churches. In other words, because of this contract we had plenty of work. We worked in ordinary non-church related design projects too, although they were not as large and generally not as plentiful in those bleak days.

One exception occurred when the legendary John Huston purchased St. Cleran's House in Craughwell in County Galway. He looked about for an architect and since we were the only purely architectural office, as opposed to architectural and engineering, in the area, Simon landed the job.

This was hugely exciting for us as we got to meet the great man and listen while he outlined his plans for the place. His first priority was to restore the steward's house and yard and then develop the stables block with a studio apartment for himself over the stables. Then he proposed to attack the main house, which is a medium sized Georgian house that had been the country seat of the O'Hara Burke family, one of whose members had been the first man to cross, almost, Australia on foot only to perish within a few miles of his objective.

The steward's house was a straightforward enough job being primarily a case of upgrading and improving the existing house so that his family could move in. When this section of the work was completed his family, which included his (then) wife Enrica Soma, a Swiss ballerina, and their children Anthony and Angelica, who are now household names in the film industry.

The next task was the development of the studio buildings and this was both interesting and sometimes exciting as Huston himself would arrive and bustle about showing us what to do and letting us know, in no uncertain terms, if we got it wrong. I seemed to get on with him fairly well, even to the extent of his giving me a present of some of his large collection of tubes of oil paint when he found out that I also painted. His relationship with Simon deteriorated though, for an unusual reason.

We were used to working for clients for whom money was a scarce commodity and were always trying to affect economies. Huston, who had just made *The African Queen,* was loaded with money that he did not want to bring back into the United States, one assumes for tax reasons, and he wanted to spend lavishly on this pet project, where he enjoyed playing lord of the manor. It came to a head over the installation of the Japanese bathroom in the cellar of the big house. Huston wanted us to send somebody to Japan to survey some examples and get the proper materials and equipment, but Simon said that we couldn't afford to go or some such and so we were paid off, only to be replaced by Patrick Scott of Dublin who was qualified as an architect but is now better known as an artist. Scott moved into the little groom's house in the stable yard and went on to spend all that was required of him. It was an interesting experience for us. There can't be too many architects who have been sacked for trying to save their client money.

Now that I was back in Galway I was able to pursue those other hobbies and sports that I had to forego while living in the country. These consisted of rugby, rowing and dancing in no particular order. Most of my mates at the time were members of Galway Corinthians Rugby Football Club. Corinthians had been founded many years before in 1932 and was based in the Galway Grammar

School, the Protestant Secondary School, formerly an Erasmus Smith College.

There were no memorable events in my life while wearing a number 4 jersey for Corinthians. Most matches in those days seem to blend into a single memory of struggling in the mud in the Galway Sports Ground with people trying to kick my head in. If there was one highlight that stood out it was the day that we defeated Old Crescent from Limerick by 33-0 in a home match. Of course to counteract this, the low light of my rugby career came soon after when we were beaten by the same team 33-0 on their turf. I was at best a less than mediocre player but I stuck it out for about four years before moving on to something a bit less humiliating.

Rowing was a different thing. I had begun my rowing career in the Jesuit College and had enjoyed it immensely, so when an opportunity came to row for a club I was delighted. The Corrib Rowing and Yachting Club was the oldest such club in Galway City, having been founded as an officers club by the British army in the 1830s. For many years from the 1920s until the 1940s it had been the flag-bearer of Galway rowing, but by the fifties rowing had died out altogether there. A few of us who had rowed for the Jes together with other lads who had rowed for other clubs came together and got a crew on the river. We began to train and work hard at reviving the club's rowing reputation, the climax of which came when we won the coveted Head-of-the-River for fours in Galway.

I also joined the regatta committee as our club's representative and for many years I was involved with the running of the Galway Regatta, which back in those days was such an important event in the city that the shops used to close for a half day on regatta day.

Rowing today is much better funded and is more competitive than it was back then; we were rowing in timber racing boats, some of which were thirty years old or more. Still I like to think that we helped to keep the tradition alive in those lean years, when many young men of our age had to emigrate just to stay alive. Of course the favourite teams to win in those days were the university senior crews and they regularly carried off the prizes. University College Galway was no exception and from time to time they were national champions. To us at that time they were as good if not better as any crew. Even though international rowing hadn't reached our shores, we were convinced that, on a good day, they could beat anybody in the world. All that changed though the week the Germans came.

We got a request from a German rowing club called Deutsch Rudergellschaft, Germania which was involved in European competition, asking us if we would allow them to come and row in the Galway Regatta. Of course we were delighted to have them come and compete here and we made arrangements to accommodate them in army beds in the ballroom of the Corrib Rowing and Yachting Club. When they arrived they were tall, handsome, fair-haired, very strong and very polite. There wasn't a man of them under six feet and unlike our crews they were, while in training, strictly teetotal.

The great day came and since this was set up as a challenge race they were pitted against the U.C.G. senior team – our crème de la crème. The start was above Menlo Graveyard, out of sight of the finishing enclosure at Oldcastle where the Quincentennial Bridge now spans the river. I was one of the finishing judges and also doing a commentary over the public address system for the large crowd gathered at the finish. Since much of the course was unseen from the enclosure I positioned a lookout with binoculars and an army walkie-talkie unit on top of the old ruined Clanricard castle that gave the area its name and another at Menlo Castle half way along the course. They were to keep me informed of the crews' progress so that I could maintain interest in the race for the crowd until they actually came in view.

The guy half way down the course said, "They're off!" as he had seen the flag raised at the start and after a few seconds he told me that the Germans had rounded the corner at the tail of the wood, still no sign of U.C.G. I of course relayed this to my crowded audience and was relieved when he said that the U.C.G. or college crew were now in sight also. It appears that the Germans had got a great start and were now about ten or eleven lengths ahead. With every stroke they seemed to pull ahead until they came in sight of my guy on the top of the castle and he said, "They are now coming up to the Iodine". Iodine was an old ruined factory about two thirds of the way along the course. At this stage the German crew were a full twenty lengths or more ahead and began to ease off on their effort. Shortly afterwards they did something that was, for me, amazingly good sport. Before they came into view of the enclosure they stopped and waited for the college crew to catch up so that they would not be disgraced. When the college crew were almost abreast of them they began to row again but really only keeping pace and when they got to the home stretch they just pulled on the power and left the college for dead. They won by about four lengths without an effort and everybody agreed that the college must have been having a bad day. Had they known the truth of the matter and had the German crew not been so sporting, they would easily have been home and had their boat out of the water before college even appeared. That was the time that I realised that Ireland was not really in the international class, something that has, thankfully, changed in the past twenty or so years.

A few years later a similar event took place when a rather arrogant Commanding Officer from Renmore military barracks who had a strong group of his men from Conamara rowing in a curragh, which is a canvas and timber six oared fishing boat adapted for racing. They were entered for the An Tostal competitions and their C.O. said that, in his opinion, there was nothing on the water as fast as them. To prove it he issued a challenge to the college senior eight rowing team over a three-mile course on the Corrib. This of course was totally foolish and ill advised, since first of all the curragh was completely out of its metier in the river and the college team had eight oars and a crew that were each pulling on one oar, while the curragh crew were pulling two oars to each of the three crew. The college offered to give them a head start but the C.O. would have none of it and so the great day came and this time, the college crew really were home and changed into their day clothes before the unfortunate curragh crew appeared. That was the last challenge of that nature that was made.

Although I am no longer involved with rowing I am still interested in it and Galway now hosts two major rowing events in the year, the Head-of-the-River in the spring and the Galway Regatta in mid summer and interest is still strong in the city even though the shops no longer close to allow their staff to attend or participate. The Corrib Rowing and Yachting Club no longer enter a crew, being now almost entirely the preserve of large motor cruisers and fishermen. But Galway Rowing Club, the Tribesmen and U.C.G. now N.U.I.G. are as involved as ever.

Apart from those sports, as I mentioned earlier, our principle pastimes were dancing and going to the pictures.

15. Strike Up the Band

—⚏—

As I have mentioned in earlier chapters, dancing was our favourite way of meeting with girls, most of whom were local and were known to us anyway and others we got to know from seeing them on the dance floor. Generally speaking we went dancing at least once a week or occasionally twice and in the summer we danced as often as we could, as the influx of summer visitors brought new and exotic women to town. During this period many of the local girls would warn us not to approach them for a dance if they were talent spotting for themselves. We all knew the drill and would only approach them if they appeared to be standing alone.

Galway had, in those days, three main ballrooms: Seapoint, the Astaire and the Pavilion, which was always known as the Hangar. The reason for this was that it had in fact been a First World War Royal Flying Corps aircraft hangar out at Oranmore flying field and after the conflict was bought by a group of local entrepreneurs and re-sited in Salthill as a ballroom. There were several decent bands; Des Fretwell's Orchestra, Johnny Cox and his big band and a family band made up principally by members of the Dooley family and known as The Arabians, but inevitably called the Arabs by the punters.

The Hangar was by far the most popular ballroom and attracted the best dancers although, because of its corrugated metal construction and low ceiling, it could be pretty hot in there even on a winter's night. It had a wonderful floor, an unbeatable, club-like atmosphere and could accommodate anything up to about eight hundred people on the floor in a crush. Many of the great visiting bands played there and dancing was always a pleasure.

The Astaire was less popular with us since it was in the middle of the city with a reputation for being a bit rougher (the odd fight was known to break out from time to time), so in general we didn't go to too many dances there. Still, though much smaller than the others, it had its own loyal following and the best local bands played there.

Seapoint was a totally different prospect altogether. It was a large, impressive purpose-built structure which still stands today, and had a ballroom capable of accommodating anything up to a thousand dancers on the floor, with room for several hundred more on the balconies which surrounded the dancing area. Downstairs there was an equally large café cum restaurant. Seapoint was the principal venue for all of the visiting big bands from England and it was possible to hear the likes of Joe Loss, Humphrey Littleton, Sid Phillips, Vic Lewis and all of the bands we heard regularly on the BBC radio. Seapoint always had its own resident band which would play in the ordinary way at the weekly dances and give support to the visiting bands when they arrived. Eventually though because of this they got into a row with the Irish Federation of Musicians, since some of the visiting bands were non-union.

The proprietor of Seapoint, Noel Finan, not one to be dictated to by any union, solved the problem by hiring his own full-time sixteen-piece non-union orchestra, producing one of the best, most swinging bands ever to grace any stage anywhere in Ireland, the Pete Roxboro Orchestra. But I get ahead of myself.

After my return to Galway and my re-involvement with every aspect of Galway City living, I became involved with a band myself.

As I mentioned earlier I had taken up the trumpet in self-defence against the piano at home and I reached enough proficiency on the instrument to be able to play for a night's dancing and would be picked up from time to time by local small bands to fill in for a missing member or just to fit up a band for a particular club dance in one of the other many smaller halls that abounded in the city.

Eventually though I took root in one of the bands; a college band run by my mate Benny O'Connor who was a drummer and who had formed the band as a way to supplement his income while he studied engineering in U.C.G. We went by the unimaginative name of The Comets, influenced in no small way by the Bill Haley band of the same name that was by now rocking student campuses all over the world with his new and exciting music, rock and roll.

The Comets were a mixed bunch when I joined them: Benny, the band leader on the drums; a medical student from Donegal called Patsy Ward on the piano; a postman from the city called Paddy Spellman on the tenor sax; one of a pair of twins called McNamara from Mayo on the alto sax and vocals; an elderly, but very experienced bass player called Bill Jones; and myself on the trumpet and vocals. We made plenty of noise, were generally in reasonable tune and kept good time, but any resemblance between us and the real rocking Comets ended there. Later our piano-playing doctor qualified and married his sweetheart Jess before they left for America. We were then joined on the piano by Martin Conneely, a blind telephonist from the Galway County Council offices and one of the best natural piano players I ever heard.

We played everywhere: in the city as well as in the countryside, in so-called paraffin oil halls and in summer in canvas marquees at many of the local carnivals. Distance was no object to us as long as they were prepared to pay. We continued in this fashion, touring the country and having a lot of fun, while holding down our day jobs, or studying as the case may be, at the same time. All was going well until we were struck by the Suez crisis.

The Suez crisis occurred between October 1956 and March 1957 and resulted in the closure of the Suez Canal by Egypt. This meant that much needed supplies of petrol could not be delivered in the

normal way and so for the first time since the war, petrol rationing was re-introduced. The allowances were dismal and were only
something like five gallons per month unless one was in a special
category of employment and so getting petrol was a major quest
before going to play at any dance.

Eventually, this became part of the fee structure of the band, if
we had to tour. The organiser of the dance had to guarantee us
sufficient petrol to get us home as well as the fee for the night if
he wanted us to play. This resulted in many a breath-taking journey home, coasting down hills and only applying power going up
hills in an effort to stretch the fuel. At the time we were driving a
mark one Ford Consul, which was a terrific car to go but like all
Fords of the time, was notoriously heavy on petrol. I recall a particular night when returning from a late night dance in Kilrush in
County Clare; the dance organiser welched on the amount of petrol we needed and could only give us one gallon. This meant that
we had to travel over forty miles on thirty miles worth of petrol
and whatever fumes were left in the tank from the journey down.
Somewhere around Gort we were showing empty on the fuel gauge
and still twenty miles from home. At one filling station we stopped
and knocked at the door of the owner's house and he told us if we
didn't get lost he'd set the dog on us. There was nothing for us to do
but carry on and we were still travelling when we hit a long climb
in the road near Kilcolgan and the engine coughed and finally just
died. There we were, with all of our gear on the side of the road,
at about three o'clock in the morning, some fourteen miles from
home. The problem for us was that we had to be at work later that
same morning at eight and we were a good three to four hours brisk
walking from home, plus we had the problem of having to carry
our instruments. When all seemed to be without solution, almost
miraculously at that hour of the morning, another set of headlamps
appeared behind us and pulled up. It was the Des Fretwell band in
their bus and while they had no petrol to spare they did offer to
crowd us into their van with our gear and so we were spared the
walk. The following day I had the job of scrounging enough petrol
to rescue the car.

On another occasion while returning from a dance in the Headford area of County Galway we were travelling along the long straight stretch of bog road, known locally as the Curragh Line, in a force eight gale with torrential rain beating down almost horizontally when Benny, who was driving thought he saw something on the road in front of us and hit the brakes. This had the effect of dislodging the roof rack with all of the gear and we watched in dismay as it all went flying into the ditch beside the road and Benny's bass drum, driven by the raging wind, went rolling merrily for a hundred yards into a large sodden bog. There was nothing for it but to grope about in the dark of the bog until we recovered all of the missing instruments set the roof rack back on and arrived home, hours later, soaked to the bone at about four in the morning.

That disillusioned us from travelling for while and we decided to concentrate on playing in the city for the foreseeable future. We were very lucky to land a most interesting and enjoyable gig in the Hangar playing as the full-time relief band for the summer. It was the job of the relief band to start the dance at eight o'clock and warm up the crowd as they came in and prepare them for the main featured band of the night. While they arrived and were performing on stage we were free to dance and enjoy ourselves the same as any of the patrons and come eleven o'clock we would play again for a half hour or three quarters to give the big band a chance for a break and when they came back we were free for the rest of the night. For us this was the dream gig and, truth to be told, we probably would have played there for nothing just for the fun of it. We played relief for many of the most popular bands of the time, including Jimmy Compton and Gay McIntyre's band from the North of Ireland, which were very popular in Galway. The other great benefit from this for us was that we were recognised by the doormen of all the ballrooms as musicians and as a result were granted free admission to all the dances on our nights off.

By far the best band of that time were the Clipper Carlton, which I mentioned earlier and we had the job of playing relief to them whenever they were in town. The proprietors of the Hangar brokered a great deal with them and got them to agree to their first and only residency, which was to play for the entire Galway Race Week. This would be similar to hiring the best known group in the country, say U2, for a full week today, as the Clippers filled any hall or venue they played in and left hundreds outside trying to get in. We knew them all very well and as a result they were happy to have us in support and we were delighted to be there.

This was our band's finest hour and something we still talk about whenever any of the survivors chance to meet. The Clipper Carlton showed the way to all of the others and changed the face of ballroom dancing in Ireland forever. Many other show-bands were to follow, based on their line up and programme; some of them national and some of them local, some of them good and some of them not so good, but I don't think that any of them since had the pure, unadulterated charisma and crowd appeal that the Clippers had back in those days. I often feel that if they were somehow to appear again on the scene today, they would lure the crowds back into the now redundant dance halls.

Towards the end of this period our band finally went the way of all bands, when Benny qualified and went on to take up his career as an engineer and the other members drifted into other bands or went on to pursue different jobs in other places. For me it had been a great time and one which I enjoyed for the whole time we were doing it and even still from time to time people come up to me and mention with fond remembrances the time when we had that band. Of course, like me, they are all getting on into their senior years nowadays, so perhaps it reminds them of a time when we were all young and carefree and life was not so stressed and driven as it is today.

Sometime in the seventies the whole business of ballroom dancing in the literal sense as we knew it, (as opposed to the fancy glittery competition style) just died out and gradually all of those great bands were replaced by disc jockeys and the large barn-like ballrooms of romance just faded away and were replaced by the discothèques, at which drinking was as much a part of the entertainment as the dancing and the dancing techniques in which one actually got to hold a girl in one's arms, such as the tango, rumba, foxtrot and waltz were replaced by a series of wild gyrations on a brightly flash-lit floor without any real contact between partners and music blaring out so loud that any attempt at conversation was futile. In this so-called disco dancing one rarely got to converse with or get to know one's partner while on the dance floor. And the fizzy lemonade or mineral disappeared into history as partners went to the bar after dancing and shared cocktails and gin and tonics or whatever was the flavour of the day.

Ironically at the start of the eighties, in my capacity as an architect, I designed Galway's first giant purpose-built discothèque out in Salthill called C.J.'s for none other than the same Benny O'Connor of my dance band days and his twin brother Cornelius at the back of their famous family pub in Salthill. This was for many years the largest and most successful disco/nightclub in the whole resort, but this too has now gone the way of all the ballrooms and discos and been demolished and replaced by apartments in the relentless march of development that is Galway today.

16. Taibhdhearc na Gaillimhe

―⁓―

Perhaps the most demanding and interesting part of my life was the time that I was a member of this illustrious theatre. I spent twenty-six years of my life virtually immersed in it and in my time there I did everything from acting to stage managing, directing, scenic designing and light and sound engineering as well as play writing. It is necessary for me to explain a bit of the history of this theatre for non-Galway readers who may not know of it.

Taibhdhearc na Gaillimhe is the National Irish Language Theatre of Ireland, situated in Middle Street, Galway. It was founded in 1928, that is to say it first opened its doors and put on a play on 27th August 1928. Its origins go back a year earlier to1927 when Dr Seamus Ó Beirn, an Irish language enthusiast broached the idea of founding an Irish language theatre similar to the Abbey Theatre in Dublin. To this end he approached the then Minister for Finance Ernest Blythe or Earnán de Blaghaid, as he preferred to be known. Blythe told him that he needed to have a committee or a company and then a venue and not least a decent Irish language play and somebody to direct it before he could consider any assistance. Back in Galway, Ó Beirn approached Professor Liam Ó

Briain and Professor Tomás Ó Máille and they began to formulate a plan to find a director and a play. Around this time the well-known Shakespearean travelling company of Anew McMaster was touring the area and Ó'Briain met up with Pádraic Ó Conaire, the well known Irish language author, who told them that there was a fine young actor touring with the company called Michael Wilmore who was McMaster's brother-in-law and that he had first class Irish and was also a playwright.

The committee decided to approach this young man and wrote to him care of McMaster's company who by now were in Limerick and invited him to come and discuss the matter with them. He replied, using his Irish name of Micheál McLiammóir and said that they would have a break on Holy Week, by which time they would be in Wexford, and asked if he might bring another young man with him who had just joined the company, a young man who was very knowledgeable in the mechanics of theatre. This young man's name was Hilton Edwards.

The committee wrote to him and invited him and on the appoint-ed day in Holy Week they arrived in Galway by train and were met by the committee. There were two halls that they needed to inspect, as these were the only two places in which they might set up a thea-tre. The first was a building owned by the Augustinian fathers that had been built only eighteen years before for social events attached to the Church. This was known as Fr. Crotty's Hall after the priest who had built it. By all accounts there must not have been much use for it as it was described as being in a run down condition. The next place they looked at was belonging to the Jesuit order and had many years earlier been a Unitarian church. It was known as the Columban Hall. Hilton Edwards, who was indeed well-versed in the practicality of setting up a theatre, assessed both of them carefully and eventually reported that the Columban Hall was the more suitable. The committee entered into negotiations with the Jesuits but after several meetings could get no proper agreement on tenancy or a lease, eventually they had to turn to the Augustinians again who apparently were a bit more amenable for they managed to agree a ninety nine year lease at a reasonable rent.

After these negotiations Ó'Briain wrote a letter to Ernest Blythe saying, "My head is spinning with the clergy and their negotiations but finally I have agreed a tenancy with the Augustinians for their hall." Blythe, who was really behind the project, when he heard that they had secured the services of an Irish language playwright and actor and now had a hall in which to begin, gave the project his blessing and more importantly, a grant of eight hundred pounds to get the show on the road. It is worth remembering that the Abbey Theatre Company who were also being subsidised by Blythe were receiving a grant of fifteen hundred pounds at the time.

After frantic cleaning, repairs and tidying the Hall was finally made ready and given the fine Celtic name of An Taibhdhearc, which was Ó'Briain's literal translation of the word Theatre. Following about five weeks of rehearsal, Mc Liammóir's play *Diarmuid agus Gráinne* was presented on stage to wide acclaim on 27th August 1928.

There was great excitement about the whole project and papers at the time hailed it as a wonderful start for a new theatre in Galway. Galway had had a pretty long theatrical tradition and the populace were well disposed to this new venture. In November of that same year a translation of Housman and Baker's *Prunella* was staged and directed by Mc Liammóir. It was around this time also that Mc Liammóir and Edwards founded their own Gate Theatre in Dublin, but Mc Liammóir continued to commute between the two as he was listed as the official director for all of the productions in 1929.

The Taibhdhearc continued in this way for the following years going from success to success with of course the odd failure and in the process developing the theatrical talents of many a young man and woman who went on to join the Abbey Theatre Company, which by now had become almost the property of Ernest Blythe as he continued to run this company for the following forty years or more.

These people included Frank Dermody, who had been a soldier in Renmore Barracks and had played the part of Diarmuid in the first play. He became the main director of plays in the Taibhdhearc in 1931, a job he held until 1938 when he left to join the Abbey Theatre Company. Following him came local Galwegian Walter Macken who became a director actor manager in 1939 and he too continued in this job until he left to join the Abbey in 1948. He subsequently became one of the best-known playwrights and authors of his time. The actress Siobhán McKenna was another very successful graduate of the Taibhdhearc in these years.

I joined the company in early 1952 where I got a walk on part in Seán O'Casey's little nonsense play *Pound on Demand* and I was smitten by the terrible theatre bug. The following year was the silver jubilee anniversary of the theatre and its company. It was decided to invite Mc Liammóir and Edwards back to do *Diarmuid agus Gráinne* again as part of the celebrations. They agreed to come, but insisted that Johnny Horan, a local solicitor who had been actor and director there for some time, would take over the nuts and bolts of the rehearsals and the play development. This was agreed and they came down from Dublin and rather poshly stayed in the Great Southern Hotel while doing the casting. This was a big step up from their humble first-floor digs in Tigh Neachtain twenty-five years earlier.

Following a week of auditions, parts were given out and I found myself cast as Goll Mac Mórna which was one of the more important parts, once Mr Mc Liammóir had checked out my legs and physique. The part required a rather vicious sword fight with real heavy iron swords against Oisín who was being played by Johnny Horan. Johnny was big into sword fights and action and was determined that this would be one of the highlights of the play and so we pounded away at each other stroke and counter stroke, night after night until it was perfect. Every night I went home with bloody knuckles and my father opined that it seemed we weren't acting but doing the real thing.

The production was a huge success and indeed the sword fight was one of the highlights of the show, which was attended on the opening night by all of the dignitaries you could imagine including the President of Ireland, Mr De Valera.

I spent the next several years doing everything from acting to stage managing, set designing, makeup, light design and general dogsbody with Traolach Ó' hAonghusa as director. In 1961 I was invited with Cyril O'Mahony to write a pantomime. Cyril, as you may recall, had been my national schoolteacher and was now the manager of the Taibhdhearc. We were firm friends and got on well together and between us we wrote our first pantomime called *TNT*. It was a great success and we were to collaborate in the writing of the pantomimes for the next three or four years. Following that I was asked to do it on my own; an invitation that gave me a chance to expose whatever talent I had as a humorous writer. In all I wrote fourteen pantomimes for the Theatre during my time there, ably assisted by another long-time member Máire Stafford who translated all of the songs we used. In 1966 I was commissioned to write and compile a show to commemorate the 1916 rising, the fiftieth anniversary of which was being celebrated that year all over the country. I was also given the job of directing it. This was called *Fornocht do Chonach Thú* and was filled with suitably patriotic music, plays and tableaux. It too was a success and apparently my directing skills were okay for I was asked to be assistant director of the panto the following year.

In 1968 I directed my first full-length play, which was *Árus Mhungo,* a translation by Seán Ó Carra of Walter Macken's *Mungo's Mansion,* which had been a big hit in the Abbey Theatre sometime earlier.

It would be too boring to continue listing all of the shows with which I was associated in some way for in all I was involved in something in the region of one hundred shows during my years there. There are some highlights though which I will take the liberty of mentioning with your indulgence. My favourite acting part was easily the most difficult part I ever played and that was the overbearing Pozzo in Beckett's *Waiting for Godot,* which we did in 1971 and again in 1972, directed by one of Ireland's most well-known directors Alan Simpson. We travelled to Dublin to the Peacock with this production and it was generally acclaimed as one of the best productions ever. Even Beckett himself was full of praise when he listened to the tape. One of my favourite plays of all time was Bertholt Brecht's play *Threepenny Opera* with the music of Kurt Weil. I had been badgering my fellow directors on the management board of the Taibhdhearc for some years to do a musical and if possible this one. Finally I was given the green light and on 20th October 1974 it hit the stage as *Opera ar Thríphingin,* a translation by Seán Ó Carra. I directed it with the assistance of Patrick Heaney as musical director and a great local jazz band called All that Jazz in the orchestra pit and the noxious beggars and whores from the cast busking the queues outside the theatre. It was a national premier and, if I say so myself, quite an achievement. To my great relief it was very well received and amongst the audience on the opening night were a few European directors, one from Holland and one from Germany who had been considering producing it themselves. This still remains the only full production of this wonderful play to be performed in its entirety, Weil's music and all, in Ireland. Although there had been pantomimes going on there for years with songs and chorus, this was to be the start of a tradition of doing a recognised musical show every year in the Taibhdhearc, a tradition which continued for many years and even branched into the realms of opera.

The other highlight of my Taibhdhearc career was known as *Seoda* and it was to become the biggest and most successful show then or since in that Theatre. It had been brought to my attention by friends that there was absolutely no summer entertainment for visitors to Galway and if they didn't want to go to the pub or the pictures, nothing else existed. For some years a group of us had been playing Irish music in a traditional music group called Ceóltóirí Chonnacht and we had achieved some success winning the Oireachtas Cabaret competition as well as the national Comhaltas Ceoltóirí Éireann Cabaret Competition several times. It occurred to me that if we could harness this into a longer two-hour show with a modicum of theatre mixed in with it, that it would be a very suitable show for tourists to Galway.

I spent some time getting a formula worked out and in 1971 presented the idea to Bord Fáilte Éireann, the Irish Tourist Board, and they agreed to give us a subvention to get the show on the stage. I then had to sell the idea to my board of directors and once assured that the show would be completely in Irish and self-sufficient financially they agreed. Truth be told they were glad to have something to put on for the summer as up to then the theatre had been dark for all of the summer months every year. Apart from the aforementioned Ceoltóirí, I rounded up a few of my favourite Taibhdhearc actors and engaged some of the most fabulous Irish dancers from the Celine Hession school, including the prima donna herself and got into rehearsal right away.

The show opened at the beginning of July that year and ran until the end of August for three nights every week and every night was a sell out. After the first year a member of the group, multi instrumentalist Pádraic Ó Carra became musical director and selected much of the music as well as playing in the group and I directed it, arranged, translated or wrote different one-act plays to fill the theatrical spot in the middle and played in the group as well. We had a great time for ourselves and we filled the house with wildly enthusiastic audiences of visitors and locals every night we were open during the entire run, which lasted for eight years.

We also toured the show to summer festivals around the country, in places like Athy and Westport and even took part of it to Germany to appear on the popular television show *Um Laufenden Bande,* where it was a huge success. In principle the show might be described as the grandfather of *Riverdance* as it showed for the first time a row of Irish dancers lined up in the manner of a chorus line, wearing sexy short skirts and dancing their hearts out, with military-like precision. The Germans gave us encore after encore and some days later, when we were leaving from Düsseldorf Airport, the people there broke into spontaneous applause, recognising the dancers although they were now dressed in jeans and sweaters instead of their dancing costumes.

By 1978 I figured that I had been in the Taibhdhearc for too long and it was really interfering with the rest of my life and in particular my architectural practice, since those potential clients who knew me felt that I was spending so much time in the theatre I couldn't still be working at architecture. For this reason I decided that it was time to bow out and so when the Golden Jubilee production of *Diarmuid agus Gráinne* came along I agreed that I would design and build the sets and do everything I could to help prepare the show for the stage, but as soon as the opening gong sounded on the first night of 15th October, I would quietly steal away across the road to The King's Head pub for a pint and to everybody's surprise, that is exactly what I did. For a while I had serious withdrawal symptoms, but in the end I got over it.

It must be understood that my work in the Taibhdhearc was on a sporadic basis, sometimes for three or four months on and off a year and sometimes much more frequently and it was done in the evenings as I had to try to get on with my actual job during the day. All of this work in the Taibhdhearc in those days was done on an amateur basis and any payment we got took the form of a cheque for maybe five pounds or ten depending on the importance of the part played. Writers and directors were paid in the region of three hundred pounds for their work and I can honestly say with hand on heart that I certainly wasn't in it for the money. Nowadays it is a professional company and everybody gets the official rate for whatever job they do.

After my resignation I got on with my business and I'm pleased to say it prospered, but I did go back once or twice to direct or write shows, but in the main my Taibhdhearc career was at an end. Funnily enough, in 2007 I was commissioned to write the Christmas panto, called *Tóraíocht an Yummy Mummy,* and it was due for production in November when a teenage vandal broke into the theatre and set it on fire causing considerable damage. They say that following repairs to the Theatre, it will be produced for Christmas in 2008.

In all I wrote some twenty plays, shows and pantomimes, directed about thirty and acted in about thirty more. I was involved in some capacity or other in about one hundred productions during my time there. Did I enjoy my time in the Taibhdhearc? I did, most of the time. Would I go back and do it all again? Not on your life!

17. Further Theatricals

—◊◊—

As well as the Taibhdhearc I was involved in much other theatrical work in Galway, not the least with the late, great Frank J. Bailey who was one of the finest young directors in Ireland.

Frank died prematurely in a road accident in 1971 while still only in his thirties and was a wonderful talent lost. At the time he was director of the Dram. Soc. (the U.C.G. Drama Society) and was born to be involved in the theatre. He ate, slept and lived the theatre and could talk about nothing else. Sometime in the mid fifties using members of the Dram. Soc. as well as a few others he founded The Galway Little Theatre Company with the dream of bringing serious theatre on a regular basis to Galway. He invited me on board as an actor and stage director and it wasn't long until we were doing two or three plays a year, this time on a semi-professional basis.

The productions were many and varied, but always skilfully done and rehearsed to the nth degree. They ranged from the plays of John B. Keane, such as *Sive and Sharon's Grave,* to international bestsellers such as Arthur Miller's *All My Sons* and Tennessee William's

Glass Menagerie. This was the first time for many years that plays of this calibre had been presented on a regular basis in Galway by a Galway Company other than the Taibhdhearc and there was a faithful, enthusiastic following for the company whenever a show was presented. We had no fixed venue of our own and the plays were performed in a variety of theatrical spaces in the city ranging form the aforementioned Columban Hall to the Grammar School in College Road. In the summer we used to travel these shows to places as far apart as Roundstone in Conamara and Castlerea in Co. Roscommon. The advance publicity was done by Tony Gill on his motorbike with Ollie Ryan on the pillion, while the travelling itself was done in a series of battered and shabby motor cars with the scenery tied onto the roof with ropes. To say that we were a rag tag outfit was fair enough in terms of our travel equipment, but we never had any complaints about the actual performances.

Touring had its problems as well as its rewards and we could find ourselves deep in trouble at the drop of a hat. I remember a particular incident that occurred in New Inn, where there was a nice little theatre that was also used as a cinema and there was also a regular audience of local country people. The trouble arose when our lead man in the production of *Sharon's Grave* left Galway to go and take up a job in Dublin as a press reporter on a national newspaper and he had to be replaced by a student actor who was in the final days of his medical studies. Doc, who has since passed away, was by way of being a local character in Galway City and although only in his early twenties sported a Mephistophelean goatee beard, which gave him a certain menacing look. He was not the actor that Seán Duignan, his predecessor, had been but was game enough to take on the part at short notice. All went well on the night until he came to the love scene, whereupon some of the local hard men down at the back of the hall began to make sounds mimicking that of a goat. Doc, who was sensitive about his beard, carried on for a moment or two until he could stand it no more whereupon he put his loved one down and said to the crowd, "We will continue with this show when the local yahoos have been ejected from the hall." At this there was uproar and the said yahoos made to storm the stage. The owner closed the curtains and suggested that we beat a retreat, which we did as fast as our legs and our battered cars could carry us. It was a week later before I plucked up the courage to go and retrieve our sets.

By far the most important production attempted was the Galway premiere of *The Importance of Being Ernest* by Oscar Wilde that was mounted as a fundraiser for the new Galway Cathedral, which was being constructed at the time. We were lucky enough to get the services of the legendary Hollywood actress Barbara Bel Geddes as our director as she was living in Oughterard and was anxious to do what she could for the cause. It was a wonderful production and she pitched in with the painting of the scenery and making of the props. The lead parts were played by Frank Bailey himself and Taibhdhearc actor Seán Duignan, with Teresa Forken and another ex-college female actor whose name escapes me as the two young things. Michael McDonagh played Canon Chasuble and the lovely bird-like Miss Prism was played by May King who was another Taibhdhearc actress. Aggie Hanley played the indomitable Lady Bracknell with gusto, while Merriman the butler was played initially by Coady Gill and latterly by me. The production was a huge success and contributed a not inconsiderable sum to the Cathedral building fund. There was much pressure on us to repeat the production as many people had heard about it and hadn't seen it and so we did it again the following year in our new home; the Dominican School Hall in Taylor's Hill. My final play with them was a murder thriller called *The House by the Lake* by Hugh Mills, in which I played a detective, to Frank Bailey's murderer.

Shortly afterwards Frank left for Dublin where he formed another theatre company in the tiny basement Eblana Theatre in the Store Street Bus Depot. Frank returned to Galway in the summer of 1971 with the idea of forming a new Galway theatre company called the Celtic Arts Theatre and he and his partners mounted an amazingly lavish production of Yeats and Synge plays in the old Town Hall Theatre, which they had booked for the entire summer run. They opened with two plays on the same night: *Deirdre of the Sorrows* and *Riders to the Sea* by John Millington Synge.

Friends, including myself, advised them that the programme looked a bit heavy and perhaps a bit gloomy for a summer season and that maybe they should have included an old reliable such as *Playboy of the Western World* in their programme, but they were not for turning and insisted that Galway was ready for serious theatre. Brilliant though the productions and the cast were, the venture bombed after a couple of nights and the whole thing collapsed. It was during the following week that Frank accidentally hit a wall in Furbo while driving home late at night and was killed instantly.

Ironically a few friends gathered around to help the cast and we were able to get the Jesuit Hall where they put on a production of *The Playboy of the Western World* for the rest of the summer. It played to packed houses every night.

My other theatrical involvement had to do with Galway's famous musical society, The Patrician Musical Society, which had been founded by Brother Cuthbert – he of the choirs in my school days – and some other Galway music lovers. The first performance was in 1953 and I was initially involved as their make-up specialist, which some nights might mean putting make-up on anything up to thirty-five or forty people. Eventually I became involved with painting the scenery with my old friend and art teacher John Mulhern and I went on later to designing the sets and the lighting and all the other stuff that I did in the Taibhdhearc including stage directing. The society, which because of Br. Cuthbert's involvement was always very strong in the chorus department, performed one show per year and in the beginning was focused on opera and light opera. Shows such as *Maritana, the Bohemian Girl, Il Trovatore,* and *The Pirates of Penzance* were amongst the early shows and were received enthusiastically by the Galway audiences. Later we became more ambitious and Grand Opera pieces such as *La Traviata, Rigoletto, Carmen, Faust, I Pagliaci* and *Cavellaria Rusticana* were performed featuring local singers such as tenor Sonny Molloy, bass baritone Gerry Glynn and sopranos Marie Geraghty, Mary Angela Coyne, Pattie Long and Pat Lillis.

If there was not a principal singer of sufficient ability to perform the lead in any of these shows, the society imported professional artists from other venues in Ireland and even from other countries to fill them. I recall a wonderful tenor David Parker from Neath in Wales in *Carmen, Pagliaci* and *Cavellaria* and baritone Russell Cooper all the way from New Zealand who sang the lead in *Cavellaria*. I spent a good few years on the committee in the sixties and like to think that I helped in some way to influence the decision to bring shows of this calibre to the city. Later, the society took a decision to concentrate on lighter and more modern musicals and as a result, the Grand Opera tradition died away, only to be revived from time to time by the Taibhdhearc Company in Irish language versions. I am pleased to say that the Patrician Musical Society continues today still doing a show a year. Who knows? Someday they may return to their classical roots. I feel that there would still be a good audience for such material in Galway today.

In the early sixties I became very interested in traditional Irish music and gravitated towards Spiddal in Conamara where the wonderfully talented Standún family were known to have sessions. It was there that I met the renowned tin whistle player Festy Conlan, who was married to Eileen, sister of Máirtín Standún. Right away we hit it off and it wasn't long before I had taught myself the rudiments of the guitar and was in the thick of it all. Ballad singing was the coming thing thanks to the arrival of the Clancy Brothers and Tommy Makem on the world music scene and since I already had a decent repertoire of 'Come all yes', as they were known from my E.S.B. days, before long I was performing at all of these sessions and having the time of my life. In the winter of 1962 driving to Spiddal became treacherous as there were plenty of icy nights and I wondered if we could get something going in Galway City. As luck would have it I attended a Jesuit past-pupils' re-union and met up with a young man called Joe Hegarty whose family owned a small quiet hotel in Dominick Street in Galway called the Enda Hotel, a venue much favoured by commercial travellers and that ilk. I told him about the sessions in Spiddal and that I was interested in getting something similar organised in Galway. (It must be realised that singing and music in pubs was greatly frowned on back in those days and if you sang in a pub you stood a good chance of being thrown out.) Joe agreed to give it a go and the following week I started the first session in the small front bar in the hotel, having first passed the word to my friends to be sure and turn up. About twenty or so mates arrived, some of them musicians also and the session was a great success. Within a couple of weeks there wasn't room to move in the bar and people were even sitting in the hall and on the stairs outside any night we had a session.

Word got around that there was this great place where you could go for a drink and there was non-stop music and craic to be had without any cover charge and it wasn't long until all sorts of people began to arrive early just to get a seat and by the time I would arrive at eight o'clock the place would be full and I would have difficulty getting a seat for myself.

Aspiring musicians and entertainers of all sorts would turn up on the chance of being given a chance to sing or perform and before long there was an amazing pool of talent on tap. There were other ordinary people who after a drink or two could be persuaded to sing, some of them for the first time in public, old songs they had learned for their parents and grandparents so it wasn't long before we built up a great store of good traditional material. The was one girl in particular called Eithne Burke who came from the Belclare area of Tuam who was engaged to another mate of mine, an A.A. man called Michael Gallen and who later became his wife. She had the greatest store of old and wonderful songs that she had learned from her father that we had never seen written down anyplace and in some cases had never even heard before. Songs like *Bold Robert Emmett the Darlin' of Érin.* And *Grá mo chroí, I long to see old Ireland free once more.* These old moving rebel songs from centuries earlier had been carried down in the vocal tradition and were not to be found in many books in those days. Of course all that has now changed and ballad books are available with hundreds of such songs, but back in those days there was not much of this material available.

Eventually playing there and even being there became very uncomfortable, such were the crowds in the front little bar in the Enda and so wearing my architect's hat I went rummaging through the out-buildings at the back of the hotel to see if we could come up with a better solution. There was a large bottling store and a fuel store side by side, both of which were in pretty good condition and made out of stone, with a strong slated roof and so I drew up plans to knock them together and build a proper traditional style old pub. Since the Planning act hadn't really taken root in the city in those days yet, we decided to go ahead with the plan and do as much of the work ourselves as possible. Together with Joe Hegarty, Eddie Ryan, Festy Conlan and a couple of lads he brought with him from Spiddal, we broke out two large arches in the party wall and reactivated a large stone fireplace which had been unused for fifty years or more. We then screeded the uneven floor and covered it with Liscannor flagstones, which were scattered with sawdust for atmosphere every night once it opened. Joe bought a large number of wooden beer barrels and we converted the large ones into a counter and medium ones into tables and the small ones into chairs and stools and on Easter weekend 1963 the Fo'castle Ballad club was born. It was a huge success and crowds flocked from all over the county to be there.

It wasn't long until the Fo'castle became one of the best-known music clubs in the country and well-known Dublin musicians such as Ronnie Drew and Luke Kelly, who were friends of Festy's, began to come down for the weekend just to join in. It would be boring to list all of the well-known performers who performed there at these sessions, but if I did it would be a list of anybody who was somebody in the folk music world. Even Paul Simon, later to team up with Art Garfunkel, did his stint there as did various and sometimes all of the famed Clancy brothers and indeed their sister Joan as the club became the biggest draw outside of Dublin for folk musicians.

For the following three years I performed there two or three nights a week. Playing there was always enjoyable and sometimes even a bit scary. One anecdote springs to mind and it is the tale of these heavy looking Americans who arrived there every night for about a week. All of them were dressed in the classic trench coats and sunglasses one sees on C.I.A. spooks in the movies. The

main man was a fairly insignificant guy but he had two big henchmen who got him his drinks and sat each side of him and made
sure nobody bothered him. They were pretty appreciative of the
programme I was performing and on the final night of their visit
one of the heavies came over and stuffed a twenty-dollar bill into
my top pocket and said, "Mr Hoffa liked you". I often wondered
afterwards what would have happened if Mr Hoffa didn't like me.
I can't swear for sure that it was the legendary teamster boss Jimmy
Hoffa, but I do know that it wasn't too long afterwards that he
disappeared, some say, into the concrete foundations of a highway
bridge in the United States.

After I left the Fo'castle, with a group of my friends, Martin and
Eamonn Rabbitte and Patsy McDonagh, I continued playing in
various other venues, which by now had sprung up all over the city,
and in particular Reilly's in Forster Street and the newly-opened
King's Head, as well as the Eagle Bar in Henry Street in which the
local chapter of the Comhaltas Ceóltóirí Éireann met on Tuesday
nights for fabulous sessions. Eventually we formed into the large
traditional Irish music group Ceoltóirí Chonnacht (Musicians of
Connacht) I mentioned earlier and we continued to play together
up until 1978.

Apart from the Fo'castle, there was another hotbed of Irish traditional music and this was the aforementioned Eagle Bar in Henry
Street in Galway. On Tuesday nights this was the meeting place
of the local chapter of Comhaltas Ceoltóirí Éireann and they had
their weekly committee meeting there. Together with a few of my
friends I was invited to join this committee and our first official
function was to propose that we no longer have committee meetings unless there was a grave need for one and that we would have a
session of music instead. This was greeted with approval by all and
sundry and from that day out there were the most wonderful Irish
music sessions there on every Tuesday night. The talent was formidable as it featured some of the best-known old time musicians
in the country as well as some wonderful up and coming players.
People like flute player Eddie Maloney of the famous Ballynakill
Céili band and fiddler Tommy Mulhaire who had a band of his

own, Jimmy Cummins on the box (accordion) together with Patsy McDonagh on the box, Padraic Ó Carra on the tin whistle and the Rabbitte brothers Martin and Éamonn on banjo and fiddle. They would be joined very often by other well-known traditional musicians from all over the county and the sessions would continue until closing time. The music could never start though until the television programme *The Fugitive* had ended, for this was the favourite programme of the proprietor Mrs Forde and there could be no interference until the hero had escaped capture for yet another week.

Radio and television programme makers always gravitated there when they came to Galway for they knew that there would be good, solid music on Tuesday nights and the renowned Ciarán Mac Mathúna made many of his best traditional Irish radio programmes for Radio Éireann there at that time.

By this time, which was the mid-sixties, traditional music and ballad singing had taken firm root in Galway and there were music sessions in almost every pub and hotel in the city almost every night of the week and the city of Galway became known as the best venue for music and craic in the country, a reputation it still holds to this day.

I think that it is worth mentioning that although I no longer play music of any sort in public, my son Richard has continued to follow in this tradition and is still playing and singing fairly regularly in some of the Galway City and County venues, with his own mates and even with some of the musicians I played with myself all of those years ago.

18. They're Gonna Put Me in the Movies

—⁓—

At the end of 1959 I was still in the Taibhdhearc when Johnny Horan, who was a director and member of the board, approached me one day. He told me that he had received a phone call from a friend of his who was involved in Ardmore Studios, Ireland's burgeoning Hollywood, who wondered if he knew anybody who was available to do set design work in an upcoming film about the famous Sidney Street uprising in London in 1911. Johnny mentioned my name and they invited me to go for an interview in the Shelbourne Hotel in Dublin on the week before Christmas. I was at the time still working for my architect boss Simon Kelly and I approached him to know if he would mind if I went. His reply was that I would be a fool not to take the opportunity and if he had been free he would have taken it himself.

Following a successful interview with the film's director Bob Baker, and the art director, the Austrian William Kellner, (well known at that time for his work on *Brief Encounter* and his Oscar nomination for *Suddenly Last Summer)* I was given the job as his assistant but told I would have to start right away. Within three days, on the day before Christmas Eve I landed in Dublin, dropped my gear into a room in the old Moyra Hotel, which is now no longer in existence, and after a quick bite to eat rushed over to a temporary studio which was a large bedroom rented in Dublin's famed Shelbourne Hotel. It was here in this luxurious room that I worked everyday and part of the nights for the next week on my own preparation of working drawings for the first four or five sets that were to be used in the film when it commenced on the first week of the New Year 1960.

For me there were mixed emotions since in the first place I was delighted and excited at having got a job in the film industry, but desperately lonely for this was the first Christmas I had ever spent away from home. Although I was living most of the time in Dublin's most luxurious hotel, I have to admit that I would have preferred to be at home especially when eating my Christmas dinner, which was delivered to my room by room service as I couldn't even afford to miss a day in the preparation of the sets.

Kellner, who was about sixty at this time, had left me the proposal sketches of the first three sets and it was up to me to detail everything from door knobs to pillar boxes, as well as prepare overall drawings for the construction team, who would be coming back from holidays (four days after Christmas) and starting to build the sets in the studios out at Ardmore in Bray. The pressure was enormous but the work itself was exhilarating and by now I was a very experienced draughtsman and also had a good few years of set design behind me in the theatre.

The following week the crew arrived and the work began in earnest. Kellner checked over my work and pronounced himself satisfied with my output and the quality of it, although he insisted that I stop drawing curves using instruments and told me to use my eye and the natural swing of my wrist. This, when I got the hang of it improved my skills no end and it wasn't long until I could draw almost perfect circles and curves with a flick of the wrist. He was a consummate draughtsman himself and we hit it off right away and I learned a lot from him during the course of the film.

Although very much what one would call a B movie nowadays, *The Siege of Sidney Street,* which was being made by Bob Baker and

Monty Berman, had attracted a veritable 'who's who?' of the British Stage and screen. The renowned stage actor Peter Wyngard played Peter the Painter, the leader of the revolutionaries, along with Tutte Lemkow, a sprightly little Russian actor/ballet dancer who played the fiddler in the opening sequences of the fiddler on the roof and Leonard Sachs, famed later as the loquacious M.C. in the wonderful variety series *The Good Old Days* on the TV, Donald Sindon, he of the deep brown voice, was one of the detectives and Irish actor Kenneth Moore was one of the villains.

The cast and the crew were a close knit bunch, most of them having worked together before, but after a few days I had settled in to the routine and the rapport and fitted right in. Surprisingly I found that once you got to know these people there was not a single prima donna or big ego in the bunch and they were all professionals to their fingernails.

We worked long hours but the pay was good and the great thing about working so hard was that we rarely had time to spend the money which just seemed to accumulate in brown wages packets in my back pocket. I was earning officially £30 per week which was about three or four times as much as I had earned in the E.S.B. and about eight times what I was earning in Simon Kelly's. Not only that but according to the union rules if we worked overtime we got time and a half, after a certain time at night we got double time and if we worked after midnight, which sometimes happened, we got double time and an extra day's pay which was a staggering amount as far as I was concerned and sometimes ran to as much as seventy pounds per week.

Such riches meant, of course, that on nights off we could all go into Dublin and enjoy ourselves. If free at lunchtime we would dine in the oyster bar of the old Red Bank Restaurant and if in town for the night our entertainment usually meant going to see the newest movie or play in town and repairing afterwards to Dublin's nearest thing to a proper nightclub in those days, The Paradiso. This was a pretty well run establishment with a proper wine cellar and waiter service and really decent food.

I hadn't yet discovered the joys of drinking in those days so in order not to appear too conspicuous I would drink tonic water with ice and lemon, which looked pretty ordinary and didn't stick out. If it had been something like Coke or orange juice I would have had to explain myself and have to answer endless question on why I didn't drink, being the only one in the company who didn't. Of course this also meant that I was in great demand as a driver. In the beginning it was a little unnerving to be friendly with and hanging out with people I had only before known on the silver screen, in particular Donald Sindon who was a very well known film actor at this time. He was hugely amusing and had an endless store of hilarious jokes, which he would tell at the drop of a hat in the big booming voice of his.

Initially I was in digs in Bray with a family called Doyle, but then I shared a house with Tutte Lemkow, a film editor called Peter Bezencenet who had been a WW2 spitfire pilot, and Jeannie Henderson, the film's dubbing editor, and there were nothing but madcap parties and games whenever we had a night off. Our house became the favourite one to visit for all of the crew and cast in the evenings. We often had anything up to fifteen or twenty in the house, sharing the cooking and the cleaning up afterwards. For a young man from the west of Ireland this was easily the most exciting time of my life so far.

Amazingly the favourite topic of conversation for people in the movie business turned out to be the movie business itself and I learned a lot about technique in discussions concerning famous shots and setups, as well as interesting techniques and ideas that had been used in films that I had seen and enjoyed solely for the plot and performance. After that time I could never look at a film uncritically, but would watch for good and bad camera angles and editing slip-ups and other little goolies like moving sets and shooting off the top of the set, stuff that rarely happens nowadays.

Almost everybody else in the business drank and not only that but drank heavily and indeed some of them could have given lessons in it. There was an old camera maintenance man called George who was inevitably so wrecked in the mornings that he couldn't drink even a glass of water such was the shake in his hands. It would fall on whoever was there to give him a shot of whiskey by holding the glass up to his lips, after which he would immediately straighten up and be perfect without a shake for the rest of the day. He also spoke with a faltering cockney accent and was difficult to understand. I found myself inadvertently replying to his conversation in a similar accent, a habit I have had for years, which comes they say from having a good ear. He overheard some of the crew admonishing me for this one day and jumped to my defence, "Naw," he said. "You lot leave 'im alone, 'ee's the only b-bloody one around these parts that I can understand". We got on like a house on fire after that. There was also a scenic artist called Gil who painted enormous life-like backdrops for the street scenes that were shot indoors in the studio. He couldn't work without at least a full bottle of gin and would never start work until everybody else had left the studio. In the morning there would be an empty gin bottle lying on the floor and the most magnificent scene painted with such accuracy that it resembled a photograph and there would be no sign of Gil again until there was another backdrop to be painted.

If we could not a find a particular prop it would have to be made and for this there was an amazing plastering studio, headed up by an old guy whose name I have forgotten but who had learned his trade as a stucco artist in Crean's of Roscommon. Sometimes we would need to build, for example, a large brick wall and Kellner would insist that the bond of the bricks had to be exactly right so as to represent Victorian London. This would entail getting the van out at night, driving about the back streets of Dublin until a suitable piece of wall could be found and then, while nobody was looking, especially the owner, the particular piece of wall would be coated with wax onto which a few layers of muslin would be stuck and rolled into the cracks, after which a coat of plaster of Paris would be applied lavishly. We had to hang about for about fifteen minutes until the plaster had set and then peel it off the wall. This would be brought back to the studio and used as a mould with which to make anything up to twenty copies which, when joined together and painted, was identical to the original wall from which it had been taken.

Many covert missions of this nature took place during the making of this particular film.

The whole business was very heavily unionised and woe betide he who would touch anything in another man's department. I recall an incident in which I nearly shut the whole shop down due to inexperience of union rules, the most militant of which was the E.T.U. or the electricians' union. The lighting bulb over my drawing board in the design studio blew one day and I was plunged into near darkness. Now I had grown up in an electrician's house and spent a number of years working for the E.S.B. and replacing a bulb was child's play to me so I stood on my stool and removed the offending bulb just as Freda Pearson, the set dresser came into the room and she let a roar at me. "Jesus Dick, what are you doing? Put that bulb back or you'll close us down." I did so but asked her what she meant and she said that only members of the E.T.U were allowed to replace bulbs and that if I rang their foreman he would send somebody. Chastened, I rang the foreman and told him I needed new 150-watt bulb fitted over my drawing board. He asked me how I knew it was a hundred and fifty watt bulb and if I had removed it. I lied and told him that I hadn't and that 150-watt was written on the bottom of it and I could read it plainly from my desk. Within about ten minutes an electrician arrived carrying a little leatherwork bag and took out a new 150 watt bulb, switched it on and said, "There you go!"

That was my swift and only lesson in militant trade unionism. I never moved any bulbs again and even to this day every time I have to change a bulb at home I am reminded of this incident forty-eight years ago. In the end it was the E.T.U that was responsible for closing down Ardmore Studios, but that is another story.

I returned to Pinewood studios with the rest of the crew at the end of the shooting of *Sidney Street* and waited there for about a month helping out in any post-production work that had to be done. The next production was a short film featuring Harry Brogan from the Abbey theatre in a Wolf Mankovitz story called *Lies My Father Told Me* and when this was finished shooting I was hired to work on another big movie called *In the Middle of Nowhere* (this title was subsequently changed into *The Webster Boy*).

By far the most exciting prospect of working on this film was working with and meeting the legendary movie actor/director John Cassavetes who was the star of this film. Working too with John Stoll who was a renowned art director was exciting and not a little intimidating, although we got on well together eventually. Stoll was the art director of *Lawrence of Arabia* and many other well-known films and was more of a hard man than Kellner had been and he pointed out to me that when I was working for him I would forget what Kellner had said and do things his way. I adapted quickly to his style of working and we got on fine after that.

The film itself was quite controversial for its day, dealing as it did with the knotty subject of homosexuality in public schools and even as we shot it there was quite some flak directed at its producer Emmett Dalton and others who worked on it. In 1960 the subject of homosexuality had not yet become the *cause célèbre* it is today. Richard Sullivan played the lead boy, while Elizabeth Sellars played the female lead. The film also featured many well-known Irish actors at the time including Niall McGinnis, Harry Brogan and Norman Rodway.

Cassavetes turned out to be a very normal and down-to-earth guy completely absorbed in what he was doing. In fact he only acted to make money so that he himself could produce and direct the sort of films he wanted to make. He absolutely loved Dublin and whenever he was free he delighted in going into town and hanging out in some of Dublin's famous bars. Since I was still not drinking I was always invited along to do the driving and we had some memorable nights out.

After that there was only one other short film which was an interview by Eamonn Andrews with Brendan Behan called *An Evening with the Quare Fella* which took about two weeks to set up and shoot, and then as suddenly as my movie career began it was over. The E.T.U got into a dispute with the management of Ardmore Studios and the place shut down. This left me high and dry and without a job for the first time in my life and I headed back to Galway to see what was in store. I knew that Simon Kelly would have taken me back because he said so, but he would have only been able to pay me about five pounds per week and having just earned an average of six or seven times this, I decided to look around for something else.

It was my mother who spotted an ad in the *Connacht Tribune* for a permanent position in the Galway County Council drawing office, which was to pay eighteen pounds per week – a not inconsiderable sum in those days. After life in the fast lane I had absolutely no desire to take a permanent job in the County Council of all places, but mother reminded me that I was unemployed and had no money so I decided to apply for the job, knowing that there was little or no chance of me getting it.

I was wrong and I got the job right away following a lengthy interview with the County Engineer, Claude Warner, who told me that it would be a very difficult and demanding job as there had never before been a full time draughtsman in the Galway County Council and that there would be a backlog of years of work to be completed. I started right away and worked like the proverbial slave for about three weeks after which time I suddenly found that there was no more of a backlog and not only that but no immediate work either and in about a month I settled into doing the *Irish Times* crossword in the mornings and the *Evening Press* crossword in the afternoon.

Unable to stand the boredom of this lifestyle, I approached other department heads to know if they wanted any work done. For one I designed a potato store for the Regional Hospital and a Judge's chair for the courthouse in Loughrea after the wickerwork one he had been sitting on collapsed and he refused to hold court until a chair suitable for the dignity of his office could be found. For the City Engineer, Redmond Lee, I designed vibrant colour schemes for much of the street furniture of the city and in particular for the seats on the promenade which up to now had always been painted green. Eventually my immediate boss got to hear of this and gave me a roasting for going around embarrassing him by looking for work after he had made a great case to the County Engineer for my appointment on the grounds that he needed a permanent assistant. Suitably chastened I returned to doing the crosswords while waiting for all of the work he promised to materialise. Of course it is worth saying that this was before the arrival of the 1962 Planning and Development Act and the subsequent need for a planning office, which was to change forever the workings of the County Council. The place is pretty frenetic nowadays and a veritable hive of industry, but back then nothing in the way of development was happening in Ireland, and I really do mean nothing. Development or anything like it was unheard of and conditions in the country as a whole were as bleak and depressing, as they had been since the foundation of the state.

The prospect of being permanent and pensionable in the County Council for the rest of my days was a pretty depressing thought and one I looked at with a sinking heart, but all of sudden, out of the blue all that was to change.

The change happened on a grey day shortly after the Christmas of 1961, when I got a phone call out of the blue from a friend of mine called Laura Browne. She said, "Hey Dicky don't you speak French?" to which I replied in the affirmative. She then told me that she had recently started working for a French company called Potez who were going to set up a factory to manufacture space heaters and they were looking for an architectural type to help, was I interested? I said that I sure was and she arranged an interview for me with her boss, one Herbert Swift Buckley.

Buckley was an American ex-soldier who was part American Indian or Native American as they are called nowadays, hence the Swift part of his name. He was brash and called me by my second name and tested my French, which I have to say was considerably better than his although a bit rusty. He seemed satisfied and told me that if I took the job I would have to go immediately to live in Paris for several months. I had to try hard not to do a little dance of joy in his office, but I said that this would not present a problem and so I went back to the County Council and handed in my notice, as far as I was concerned I had landed on my feet again.

Potez was one of the first of the new factories that were supported by the Irish Development Authority or the I.D.A. under the leadership of the new Fianna Fáil Taoiseach Seán Lemass. Lemass's ambition was to turn Ireland into a manufacturing country with the ability to keep the workforce in the country and boost the economy and bring Ireland into the twentieth century. In truth he was right and as events were to show, Ireland really did get up off its backside and begin to develop under his management and there are those who still say that the economy of Ireland started to climb for the first time under Lemass's stewardship.

19. Gay Paree!

—∿—

At this stage I was just twenty-five and I think it fair to say that every young man of that age should have to spend a year in Paris. I couldn't believe my luck; as I arrived by taxi to my hotel I found that I was actually holding my breath in excitement.

The Potez Company was a large industrial concern that manufactured oil-fired space heaters for homes, offices and apartments, as well as very, very sophisticated aircraft. Their Potez Fouga, later to become known as the Fouga Magister was one of the first serious operational jet fighters to be purchased by the Irish Government. They had two major factories, one in Dreux and the other in Evreux as well as offices at Suresnes and at 46 Avenue Kleber. This address was in the most fashionable district of Paris – the sixteenth, where anybody who was anybody had their apartments or houses.

I was lucky in that I was to be based permanently in the Avenue Kleber office, which was the head office. The company was still presided over at that time by the elderly Henri Potez, a First World War ace fighter pilot. In fact the company logo was the *cigogne* (stork), which had been the logo of his escadrille in that conflict. We got on like a house on fire and although he was probably seventy at the time and I a callow youth, in our leisure time we were never done talking about First World War planes and flying aces. The fact that I could speak reasonably fluent French and was an aeroplane nut helped a lot in cementing this friendship. His son Gerard, who was a different kettle of fish entirely as he was set more in the playboy mould, assisted Henri in this enterprise.

I was placed in the Hotel Sylva in Rue Pergolese not far from the Arc de Triomphe and every morning I had to walk to the office past the Paris headquarters of Interpol where spooks in sunglasses would come and go as I passed; the racing garage of the Porsche Team from which the most magnificent sounds and smells of high revving racing cars emanated; and the apartment of Maria Callas, where I always hoped to meet the Diva in person, but never did.

Not long after I arrived, following Sunday mass in the Église St. Joseph in Avenue Wagram, which was the base of the Irish Passionist Fathers, I discovered that they operated a sort of club in a building attached to the church, which was aimed at the English-speaking youth resident in Paris. Part of their mission in Paris was to keep an eye on young people of any persuasion who were living away from home in the hope that they could be prevented from falling into the many pitfalls which this mighty city was known to have. They had a small English language library, occasionally the most up-to-date Irish and English newspapers and facilities for making tea and coffee and even some light snacks. It was a place where young people could meet and hang out for a couple of hours each evening. I dropped in and met some of the regulars, many of whom had been living in Paris for some years and others like myself who had only just arrived.

I recall two girls in particular, Callie McGrath and Anne McErlaine, who bore a passing resemblance to Jackie Kennedy, both of whom worked, as far as I can recall, in the Irish Embassy at the time. There was an English-speaking young Greek called Xavier Bilcox and another English girl called Jo Wainwright, as well as an ancient Irish republican, called Joe something, in a black beret who had been on the run some years earlier in the North of Ireland and an American teacher called Rick. Of course there were many others but these I mention formed the kernel of the crowd I was to hang out with during my time there.

At that time Paris attracted lots of young people, girls in particular, who were drawn by the colour and the excitement of living in this most glamorous of cities. Many of the girls were Irish and working as au pairs and often unwittingly found themselves slaving for French or other foreign families who treated them like absolute dirt and thought nothing of having them mind their children for twenty-four hours a day, seldom giving them time off, hardly paying them at all and actually in some cases not giving them enough food to live on. These were the ones that the club was set up to protect and as far as I could see they did a great job.

Around the corner from the club was a bar called La Flamme and it was to there we used to repair after our sessions at the club. The barman in this most comfortable of pubs was a little Spanish Basque called Jojo and he knew everybody and they him. Whenever I wanted to go out for the evening I would walk over to La Flamme to see who was there and within half an hour there would be some of the gang who would turn up or maybe even all of them.

The first time I ever took an alcoholic drink was shortly after my arrival in Paris when I was lunching with some of my work colleagues and I tried a glass or two of wine. Lunch with our colleagues always ran to a couple of bottles of wine at least and I often went back to the office feeling the great warm glow and I found that it was not uncommon for my workmates to have a little siesta in their offices after lunch. This was not frowned on and was considered quite normal as long as it was not abused.

For most of my life I had been a jazz nut and now I found myself in the home of some of the best jazz musicians in the world. At night, having picked up a friend or two from the bar, we would go to one of the music bars or clubs that abounded in every quarter. One such club, which comes to mind, was La Cigalle not far from the famous Moulin Rouge in Pigalle. A swinging sax player called Al Livart headed up the house band and it was one of the most progressive around. It was possible to hang around and listen to this most creative group of musicians over a couple of beers for the whole evening, something we did on a fairly regular basis.

A little later I discovered that the great Sidney Bechet's band, which at that time had been taken over by his sidekick Claude Luther, was playing on a regular basis in a place called Le Slow Club on Rue de Rivoli. Luther, who was one of the best known jazz musicians in France, like Bechet, played the soprano saxophone and kept strictly true to the bands traditions (he was the one that wrote the classic *Petit Fleur).* We sought it out and it turned out to be a speakeasy type club down about two or three floors underground in what were old wine cellars. The smoke was so thick that it seemed like a permanent fog, the lighting to say the least was minimalist but the music was divine. Tune after tune of my all time Dixieland and blues favourite were played by this magic band, which had lost none of its terrific sound at the takeover by Luther. We went there on a very regular basis and it never failed to impress. Eventually they got to know us all there and would sometimes play a piece for *Les Irlandais.* It was common for local musicians to drop in and jam with the band and some nights the group would swell from its original six to any thing up to twice that number. I would have given anything to join them but didn't have enough skill for such exalted company, or so I thought, until one night when I was a little bit jarred, some of my mates borrowed a trumpet and handed it to me. I picked it up and, knowing the drill, waited beside the stage until I was invited up. I was invited to lead off and I started with the only real blues number I knew well enough to play in such company, *Basin Street Blues,* and within seconds the whole place was throbbing to the blues. Somebody else started off the next set and I quietly joined in, then in the spirit of quitting while I was ahead I returned to my seat with the applause of the crowd and particularly my mates ringing in my ears. I would say that this for me was certainly one of the most memorable nights of my life.

No matter how long I was in Paris I never lost the sense of awe at just being there and whether it was visiting the Louvre or just sitting in a café in the sun drinking coffee watching the world go by in the manner of the Boulevardiers of old, I was in my element.

One night a group of us were celebrating Xavier Bilcox's birthday up in a Greek restaurant cum bar in the Montmartre region. We had consumed not a little wine and a good few ouzos as well and there was a lot of Greek dancing and music going on. In our company was a colleague, a man from Wexford called Tom who had been hospitalised for a few days as a result of leaving his window open in his Dreux hotel and had been severely bitten by mosquitoes. Tom had been sent up to Paris for a bit of R and R and although he was still not completely recovered he was on the right side of a few beers. I should mention that he was a tall handsome man of the George Clooney type and was, quite unknown to himself, attracting the attention of all of the women present.

Suddenly the door opened and one of the most beautiful blonde women I had ever seen came in and, without looking left or right, approached him, linked his arm and tried to get him to leave with her. Tom, who had little or no French, turned to me and asked what she was saying and I replied that she had a large limo outside the door and was trying to take him home to bed. With that Tom pulled away from her and told me to tell her that he was a happily married man, which I did. This only seemed to increase her fervour and she grabbed him again; this time tried to shove him out rather than drag him. Again he told me to tell her to get lost that he wasn't interested but she didn't want to know. Finally he said very slowly and distinctly that if she didn't leave him alone he would effing belt her one and a few of us intervened in case he might do just that. Many of the other men in the bar offered her their services, but she just spat at them, stalked out to her limo, slamming the bar door on the way. Apparently she was an extremely well to do lady who had just divorced the year before and was known to frequent this and other bars in the hunt for a partner for the night. I think Tom dined out on that story for many a year after that – I know I certainly did.

Life in Paris wasn't all fun and games and I did have to work pretty hard preparing working drawings of the typical installation methods for the Potez heaters, that and inspect all of the tool drawings to make sure that we had everything we needed in a brand new factory to build and assemble the heaters. As well as this I had to talk to the various machinists and find out from them what the snags were in the production methods so that the same problems wouldn't happen to us when we got started. My notes concerning these matters filled two very large notebooks that were almost as thick as a telephone book. I'm sorry to say that when we returned to Ireland, these books gathered dust on the top of my desk as nobody in management wanted to know anything about the problems. Until they occurred on our own assembly line that is and then they, the bosses, wanted to know why they hadn't been told about these problems. Such is life in middle management.

At this time there was considerable danger in Paris as they were in the middle of the OAS terrorist crisis. The OAS was a secret army in the manner of the IRA, but potentially much more lethal as it was made up of dissident French army officers and men, including ex-members of the French Foreign Legion who were bitterly opposed to independence for Algeria. They embarked on a reign of terror including random bombs, assassinations and general mayhem. General de Gaulle, convinced that they were going to stage a coup d'etat and try to take Paris, ordered tanks onto the streets and there were a few uncomfortable days and nights, but eventually reason prevailed and they were returned to barracks. Nevertheless there were several plastic bomb incidents in the city; I recall one about two blocks away from our hangout that exploded in a travel agents shop and blew the large glass window into the street, blinding a young female student who was passing at the time.

During this madness I was passing along a narrow street one evening on my way to the club when I spotted a Simca car, which was riddled with bullet holes in the manner of the Bonny and Clyde movie. It was parked against the kerb not far from a police station, which during those days had sandbag barricades built outside their main entrances. Being by nature curious I had to stop and have a look and then, to further stick my nose in, I went over to the policeman whose head and shoulders I could just see over the sandbags to ask him what had happened. He said nothing but swiftly brought up a machine gun, which he had been holding out of sight, and pointed it straight between my eyes. It was plain to me then that this was none of my business and that this man was a sentry on duty outside the station. I courteously bade him goodnight and continued on my way with my knees wobbling and resisting the terrible urge to run until I got around the corner and was free to breath easily again. That was the last time I ever went near a Paris policeman, it was also the last time that I took that route on the way to the club.

All good things have to come to an end and it wasn't long until I had to abandon my happy Parisian life and friends and head back to Galway where the factory was now under construction. Around this time there was a campaign going on to try to attract skilled Irish men who were working in heavy industry in England to come home and, following the Galway Races, when most Galway men came home on holidays in those days, we set up a special hiring fair in the shell of the factory. I was given a caravan in the middle of the factory floor while other management figures had offices and sometime just tables and a couple of chairs at which to interview the hundreds of men who turned up. Many of these men had been working in the motorcar factories in Coventry and Luton and couldn't believe their good luck to find similar jobs back in their own hometown.

It wasn't long until the factory was in full swing staffed by highly experienced workers who were getting a decent wage; it looked as if Seán Lemass's ideas were paying off.

20. Storms and Marriage

—ᴍ—

In September of that year Galway was struck by a most ferocious hurricane. Known as Debbie it arrived one Friday evening/Saturday morning and when the wind gauge machine at the Black Head weather station blew apart it was recording winds of one hundred and forty seven miles per hour (236 kph). This terrible wind tore through Galway City scattering roofs so that huge heavy slates were flying like confetti and trees, which still had their foliage on, fell like ninepins. Such was the wind that it was not possible to stand erect and I recall catching an old lady, who had braved the wind and gone out to the butcher's shop, as she blew past me like a piece of tumbleweed.

Such was the ferocity of the storm that there was hardly a single roof in the city which did not suffer and the building contractors made hay for the following months as they set to repairing the damage. One enterprising roofing specialist Tommy McLoughlin spent the day building new roofing ladders and by the time the wind had died down he had deposited something in the region of twenty of them on various damaged roofs about the city thereby claiming them for himself in the manner of the old pioneers staking out claims in the Wild West.

Two weeks after that I was married to my long-time fiancée Irene. We had been engaged for some time but, as is sometimes the nature of these things, it was off and then on again a couple of times. We decided that the time had come to stop procrastinating and we were married in Galway on 30th September 1961.

It is not my intention in this book to go into the ins and outs of our marriage but within three years we had two wonderful children, a son Richard and a daughter Derval. If I say that they were the most positive and blessed things that happened to us in the course of our marriage, I can do so with my hand on my heart and without fear of contradiction from any quarter. The marriage was to fail but we waited by mutual consent until our daughter Derval had finished with her secondary school education before parting after twenty years of marriage. We parted without acrimony and in 1982 had a judicial separation, followed a few years later by a church annulment and as soon as it became available in Ireland, a no-fault divorce.

We have remained good friends and both she and I married the people that we had loved in private for a long time. Following the church annulment I married the love of my life Dorothy in Craughwell Church, however the marriage though recognised by the Church was not legal and so, following the arrival of divorce in the Republic of Ireland, she and I were married yet again, legally this time by the local registrar. It is fair to say that both my first wife and her partner Pat, and Dorothy and myself have lived happily ever after, maintaining an excellent relationship with everybody concerned.

Working for Potez was interesting and exciting for the following two years but in 1963 John F. Kennedy dropped a bombshell in Europe that was to wipe out the Irish company. The factory had primarily been set up to open trade with the Balkan states, which were part of the U.S.S.R. But Kennedy laid down the law and said that as part of the Cold War any state that was a member of NATO would be forbidden in any way to trade with Iron Curtain countries. Now Ireland wasn't a member of NATO but France was at the time and the parent company was selling jet planes and all sorts of stuff to NATO countries so they decided to shut down the Irish plant.

This was a great pity as the factory had by this stage sent several ship loads of heaters to Yugoslavia and Czechoslovakia and was still churning them out at the rate of about 300 per day.

I was sent to England in March of that year to set up a stall at the Ideal Homes Exhibition at Olympia in London in an attempt to open up the English market. Even though I sold thousands of heaters and got some great contracts with major Irish owned companies there, it wasn't enough. On my return to Galway in spite of my success in selling so many heaters I got into a row with Buckley as he refused to refund the £4 for my taxi to the airport at Heathrow because I was too late to get the bus. This was not my fault as I had been forced to stand my ground at the exhibition waiting for a French lady who had been supposed to take over from me but went shopping in London instead. Buckley was not used to anybody standing up to him and he began to threaten me, so I told him that I was off, not really knowing where I was going to go and now having a family to support.

Kismet struck again however and while I was clearing out my desk the phone rang and it was Ralph Ryan the owner of the biggest engineering and architectural firm in the city. He asked me if I would be interested in running the architectural office of the company and without hesitation I said yes. Ryan's was primarily an engineering company with huge contracts for public works all over the country ranging from jobs such as the deepening of Galway Docks to the building of the bridge to Valentia Island off Kerry and large water and sewerage schemes all over the country.

The architectural side of the business was much smaller and for a while just consisted of an assistant draughtsman and me. Later we were joined by architect/engineer Mick Quaide and the amount of work grew. One of the regular jobs that we in the architectural section got to do fairly regularly was checking out buildings which were the subject of applications for mortgages from both the Irish

Permanent and Educational Building societies, as Ryan had the franchise from both. It was while carrying out one such inspection that I met a young man from Garrafrauns in County Galway who was building two houses. The young man, who was called Martin Hession, told me that he had come to Galway to make his fortune and said that he intended to be a millionaire before he was thirty.

A year later I was working for him and his partner Johnny Dooley, an engineer and former international rugby player for Ireland, designing and building three of the largest housing estates in the city; Greenfields, Highfield Park and Whitestrand Park as well as several apartment blocks and office blocks and the largest pub in Galway, The Castle Inn. I was to stay working with this company for three years until they ran out of things for me to do and so for the first time, in 1967 I began working for myself in my own small architectural practice and continued to do so for the next 35 years until my retirement in 2002.

I specialised in bars and shops and one-off housing and built a few decent buildings in my time, many of which have been knocked down in the intervening years and replaced with bigger and better buildings in the modern race to develop every inch of the town and county. Perhaps the most notable job was the building of the Corbett Court Shopping Mall, the first such enclosed mall in the west of Ireland; this was later added to and now incorporates the Eyre Square Shopping Centre. I also designed what has been described as Galway's prettiest building and the one that is the most photographed by tourists to the city. I refer to The Treasure Chest which is also Galway's classiest store run by the amazing Mary Bennett, one of the most dynamic in Galway or in any other city in Ireland. It would be dreary to continue listing job after job, but I should point out that in general I enjoyed most of my life working for myself, even though there were lean times as well as good times.

The worst time of all came in 1983 when all of a sudden, without a warning, the whole business just collapsed, not just for me but also for every architectural practice in the city. For several years things had been buzzing along buoyed up by the apparently strong economy and during this time there were three large architectural practices in the city and three small ones and there was apparently work for us all, but once this depression arrived all of the big offices began shedding great numbers of their staff to keep their costs under control. Unfortunately all of the architectural staff that was let go drifted into the small-practice pool and suddenly there wasn't enough work to keep any of us going.

For a long time I had wondered how I would do if I gave up and tried to make a living as a writer and now, out of work, I decided that the time had come for me to try. I decided too that it had to be a clean break, so after a discussion with Dorothy I felt that the solution was to sell up everything here and head for France. We had many friends in the south of France in Provence, with whom we had stayed on holidays and who had holidayed here with us, so we contacted them and told them of our plan and they invited us to come and stay with them until we could find a place of our own.

Within a short time I sold my house and paid off all of my debts, put into storage anything I couldn't carry in the VW camper van I had bought for the move and, without further ado and hardly looking back, we headed for France. It was still winter when we got there in early 1984 and we very soon found out that the heater in the old VW left a lot to be desired as we drove through snow storms through the mountain passes of the Massif Central. True to their word our friends Hugue and Nicole offered us accommodation and before long we had found a place of our own in the village of Sarrians about halfway between Orange and Carpentras in the Vaucluse.

The house we found was an amazing old farmhouse called La Grange Basse and it was perfect for what we wanted. There were two or three reception rooms and about three bedrooms with two staircases. Best of all there was an old conservatory at the back of the house and it was here I set up my office. Because funds were limited at the time I decided to get on with the writing as soon as I could. I set up my big electric IBM golf ball machine on an old kitchen table pulled up a chair and within a couple of days I was embedded in a novel concerning a young man from Galway who had been working for several years returning to his native city for the Galway races. The working title was *Home for the Races*.

My work plan was one I had learned from the late, great Galway author Walter Macken, who had told me that writing was like any other job and the only thing to do was to sit at your typewriter first thing in the morning and stick at it until lunch time and again in the afternoon until about four when you should stop and read what you have written. He didn't believe in sitting around waiting for the muses to visit; he said it was like digging a ditch, pick up your shovel and start digging and in the afternoon you can look behind you and see a ditch. If it wasn't the sort of ditch you wanted you could always tidy it up later.

This made sense to me and so every morning, at about nine, after breakfast I would start banging away at the typewriter and Dorothy would arrive with a cup of coffee at about eleven and just leave it on the table. We would break at about twelve thirty for lunch, take a little siesta for about an hour, and I would begin again at about two and continue for another two or, if I was on song, maybe three hours. Then I would stop and together we would read it and Dot would proof it and make suggestions. So now I was a full-time writer but without the prospect of any money so far.

That changed when I got a call from a friend on the celebration committee for Galway's Quincentennial, which was Galway's big thing that year. He wondered if perhaps I might write a play pageant on the history of Galway which would be presented as part of the celebrations in Galway's oldest venue, St. Nicholas Collegiate Church. I was delighted of course and immediately put the book aside and began working on the enormous play pageant *Where Once Stood Tribesmen*.

Getting the ideas for the script together and typing it out was pretty frenetic for several weeks but finally it was ready and I posted it (no e mails in those days) to Galway. To my great relief they liked it, although they did employ another writer to extend it past the late mediaeval period (in which I had finished it) up to the near present. Galway's most famous living director Gary Hynes of

Druid directed it and by all accounts it was a great success. More importantly a nice cheque arrived in the post and I was able to get back working on the novel. This progressed until one night in bed I got this terrific idea for a play about a brother and a sister, former gentry, living in an alcoholic haze in the basement of their ruined mansion. I scribbled a few notes down on the notepad I always keep at the side of my bed and went to sleep.

The following morning I couldn't resist getting started on this play so I set the novel aside once again and began working at high speed on this new play, which had the working title *Auld Dacency*. After several weeks the first draft was finished and I thought that it would work well, so I refined it and sent it off to a few theatrical companies I knew, in particular Druid in Galway and the Abbey Theatre in Dublin. I decided that I might as well aim high. When this was done I went back again to the novel.

By now well over six months had passed and I felt I had been fairly productive, but in spite of that there was no money coming in. We had really enjoyed living here in this wonderful environment, but the funds were running out. Around this time our friends asked us if we wouldn't mind house-sitting for an artist friend who was going away for a couple of months and we said, "Sure", so we moved into the former 16th century abbey of Caderousse which was to be our home, free from rent, for the next couple of months. It was an amazing house and we used to have our lunch and dinner in the garden, which had been the former cloisters of the Abbey. I continued to batter away at the typewriter, but the funds were getting lower and neither of us had any prospect of earning any money as we wouldn't be allowed to work there without registering as residents and going through a huge amount of red tape. For our last month we were house-minding yet again – this time for the parents of our friends, who had gone off on a cruise. Finally we decided that before we were penniless we should head back, as Dorothy was still employed at U.C.G. and had only taken a year's career break. We packed up the van and the car, for we had purchased an old 2CV Citroen shortly after arriving so that we wouldn't have to use the camper when travelling everywhere.

We arrived at my mother's house in Dublin for a couple of days visit when we disembarked from the ferry in Rosslare and the first thing she told me was that there had been somebody from the Abbey Theatre trying to contact me on the phone. I called the number back and it was my old friend Christopher Fitzsimon for whom I had previously written *The West's Awake,* a compilation of Western Irish writing which had been performed in the Peacock Theatre. Chris told me that the Abbey wanted to do my play (Kismet strikes again!) and would I be able to come in and discuss it with them? Would I ever? The following morning I was there bright and early and following a most interesting meeting with Christopher and the artistic director at the time, Joe Dowling, I left with a contract and – more importantly – a nice fat advance cheque in my hot little hand.

In November of that year the Abbey Theatre Company, starring Joan O'Hara, Niall Behan, Donal Farmer and John Olohan, performed *Auld Dacency* in the Peacock Theatre, under the direction of Ben Barnes and it was proclaimed a success by almost all of the critics. As far as I was concerned, thanks to the play, I was now pretty solvent again for the time being and, no matter what the begrudgers said, I could count myself in the ranks of the Abbey playwrights.

The amazing thing was that once I returned I found myself greatly in demand again as an architect, thanks to the arrival of the section 23 tax breaks which gave enormous tax concessions for the development of derelict sites and before long I was busier than ever before. In 1996, a reworking of the play was performed to critical acclaim by Punchbag Theatre Company in the Galway Arts Festival as a feature play with the name of *Dance of the Dinosaurs.* Eventually in 1998, after fourteen years, the *Connacht Tribune* publishing group published the novel *Home for the Races.* So all in all the experiment had worked, although I certainly hadn't become rich as a result, but for me there was the artistic satisfaction.

I might have continued in architecture for a year or two more after my retirement in 2002, except for the lunatic planning process now in place in the Republic of Ireland, which is a veritable minefield of problems, eco warriors and changing regulations, as well as planners with little or no appreciation of architecture and who vary from person to person in their interpretation of the rules and who often impose nasty little unwarranted conditions of their own, with absolutely no architectural qualifications, to sometimes ruin perfectly simple proposals. In the U.K. the planning process is there to help one with their developments in a positive and ordered way, in Ireland the planning offices, many of whom don't even employ an architect, appear to be there specifically to hinder and prevent any development and even when they do pass something, it can be objected to by any number of eco warriors or just busybodies and even after all that if it is still passed it may have to run the gauntlet of organised public protests in the name of democracy which in reality is anarchy rather than democracy.

I am glad that I am not starting out in this business today and I am also glad that the E.S.B. managed to carry out rural electrification when it did all those years ago, for they wouldn't stand a chance of doing it today, as there would be protest marches in every village and townland with eco warriors, NIMBYs and the lunatic left objecting to every single one of the poles.

21. Learning to Fly Yet Again

—ᴍ—

My father died in January 1976 in his seventieth year, quietly while watching Match of the Day on television. I mention this because it released me from a promise I had made to him almost thirty years before. I had gone for a couple of flights in the early fifties with a couple of the members of the nascent Galway Flying Club and even had a couple of lessons from the renowned Captain Darby Kennedy from Leixlip, who used to fly down from his airfield in Weston give lessons out at Oranmore to intending students and fly home to Weston again in the afternoon. Captain Kennedy also had a delightful daughter Rosemary who not only gave lessons but also was a parachutist, a daring and glamorous occupation back in those days. My father found out about these lessons and became really upset for he had an enormous fear of flying and begged me to promise that I wouldn't do it while he was alive as he was afraid of losing his only child. I tried to explain that flying was relatively safe nowadays but he would hear none of it, so reluctantly I agreed to promise him as requested.

In March of the following year I was in a position to be able to afford lessons and already one or two of my friends had begun to fly. Following a trip with a good friend Peter Greaney one fine Saturday morning, I decided that there was now nothing to stop me from having a go myself. I took my first fifteen-minute lesson on 22nd March in the club's only airplane, a Cessna 150 with the call sign EI-ATH or Tango Hotel. I was hooked and the following month I had an accumulation of over two hours, half an hour the following month and a massive three hours in June. I got my student pilot's licence on 29th June and on 7th July I flew my first solo following a total of six hours instruction.

I still find it difficult to describe in words the absolute exhilaration tinged with a modicum of fear and a lot adrenaline that I felt when our senior instructor Tom Tuffy said to me, "Stop here on the runway Dick, now wait a minute until I get out and off you go on your own for a couple of circuits and for God's sake don't break the aeroplane".

Taxiing back along that runway on my own for the first time in this beautiful little aircraft, I could hear my heart pounding louder than the roar of the engine and following the usual preflight checks I shoved the throttle home all the way. Within seconds I was airborne with nobody to tell me what to do and nobody to blame but myself if anything went wrong. It was a scary feeling as well as an exhilarating one and strangely I found myself thinking of my late father as I climbed out of the airfield and could see the whole of Galway Bay stretching out before me.

After another fourteen months, in June of 1978 I qualified for my full pilot's licence having accumulated some 51 hours flying, 31 of those solo. The only problem in getting my pilot's licence was to pass the pretty severe written exam which was held at the Aviation Department in Dublin and although I was pretty up to date with all of the subjects, there were some pretty difficult papers to pass, not the least of which were Air Law and Meteorology. To get through this, my friend P. J. Greaney agreed to accompany me to Dublin and we spent the night before the exam boning up on the possible question with P. J. asking them and I having to answer them. As it happened on the day I went through the papers fairly easily, even through the Met paper, which was as difficult as predicted. Thanks to our boning session I knew the answers to most of the questions. I was one of only a handful who passed the Met paper out of 32 entrants. Now I was free to fly when and where I liked and to carry passengers if I wished.

A couple of weeks after this I had my first flight on Yankee Bravo EI-AYB, a beautiful French aircraft called a Gardan Horizon which was a fully retractable four-seater, very slick and might have been called a sports car of the air. Four of my mates including P. J. Greaney and I had purchased this aircraft previously, but because it was more complicated than the aircraft we were used to, we appointed a local professional pilot, Hayden Lawford as our instructor on the aircraft type and agreed that none of us would fly it until passed by Hayden. I was the first to be passed and I took to the air for my first solo flight in this wonderful aircraft on 31st August 1978.

It would be boring to non-aviation readers to continue with all the flight details but the aircraft enabled us to go when and where we wanted and I flew my first international flight, if it can be called such, from Galway to the Isle of man for the TTs the following June.

Unfortunately during the collapse of my business mentioned above in 1983, we were reluctantly forced to sell the aircraft and, although I did a fair bit of flying at Plain de Dieu in France while we were there, when my licence ran out in 1986 I never renewed it. Unfortunately, if one is five years without a licence it is necessary to start all over again from scratch to renew it and, while I might make it again, the urge isn't as great as it was and although I still have a great interest in flying and aeroplanes, I just have to file it away as one of my more enjoyable memories.

When I gave up flying I decided to dabble at another of my long-time passions, old motor cars and have been the proud possessor of a few over the past twenty years or so. I enjoy just puttering around with them, picking at this, cleaning that, tuning the other and when they are working properly, we compete in local and national rallies. My current liability is a 1919 Buick Tourer that resembles a Model T on steroids to look at, but is wildly temperamental. In this monster we have competed in the famous Gordon Bennett vintage rally on a number of occasions. It sits in the garage now most of the time because I find that since we retired we seem to have much less time on our hands than we did when we were working full time.

Nowadays our time is divided between our house in Craughwell, Co Galway and a little retirement home we bought in Puisserguier in the Languedoc in the south of France. We were fortunate enough to find it and to be able to afford it at the time and now we spend anything from three to four months a year in that most beautiful part of the world. We have a little vineyard there of about half and acre (.2 hectares) which contains about 650 vines which produce anything from 600 to 1000 kilos of grapes. When these are delivered to the local co-op we end up with enough delicious wine to last us for the year.

We spend time in the spring pruning them and fertilising them, the summer making sure that they are free from disease and usually in September, together with our neighbours and a few other Irish vigneron mates, we form a meitheal to pick ours and theirs and transport them by tractor to the co-op.

For us this is the realisation of a dream and we consider ourselves lucky to have survived in reasonably good health (in 2003 I contracted lung cancer which was speedily and totally cured, thank God and a wonderful medical team) to enjoy this wonderful life.

Would I do it all again? Probably, well most of it, have I any regrets? Very, very few.

Dear Reader

I hope you have enjoyed this publication from Ballyhay Books, an imprint of Laurel Cottage Ltd. We publish an eclectic mix of books, ranging from memoirs by Hugh Robinson, Aideen D'Arcy and Viv Gotto to histories of local events and institutions by John O'Sullivan, Harry Allen and Ivor Edgar. Lovers of local music will enjoy Jackie Boyce's compilation of folk and traditional songs, while readers with an interest in poultry will find *Roosters and Hens for the Appreciative Eye* a most entertaining and informative read. *The Donegal Currachs* by Donál MacPolin initiated an aquatic theme, now joined by *In the Wake of Giants* the latest title to join the collection.

To see details of these books as well as the beautifully illustrated books of our sister imprint, Cottage Publications, why not visit our website at www.cottage-publications.com or contact us at:–

Laurel Cottage
15 Ballyhay Rd
Donaghadee
Co. Down
N. Ireland
BT21 0NG
Tel: +44 (0)28 9188 8033

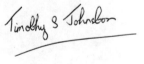

BALLYHAY BOOKS